NATURE

Divine Experiences with Trees, Plants, Stones and Landscapes

Enjoy these other books in the Common Sentience series:

ANCESTORS: *Divine Remembrances of Lineage, Relations and Sacred Sites*

ANGELS: *Personal Encounters with Divine Beings of Light*

ANIMALS: *Personal Tales of Encounters with Spirit Animals*

ASCENSION: *Divine Stories of Awakening the Whole and Holy Being Within*

GUIDES: *Mystical Connections to Soul Guides and Divine Teachers*

MEDITATION: *Intimate Experiences with the Divine through Contemplative Practices*

SHAMANISM: *Personal Quests of Communion with Nature and Creation*

SOUND: *Profound Experiences with Chanting, Toning, Music and Healing Frequencies*

Learn more at sacredstories.com.

NATURE

Divine Experiences with Trees, Plants, Stones and Landscapes

Featuring

ANA MARIA VASQUEZ

Sacred Stories
PUBLISHING

Copyright © 2022 All rights reserved.

This book or part thereof may not be reproduced in any form, stored in a retrieval system, or transmitted in any form by any means-electronic, mechanical, photocopy, recording, or otherwise without prior written permission of the publisher, except as provided by United States of America copyright law.

The information provided in this book is designed to provide helpful information on the subjects discussed. This book is not meant to be used, nor should it be used, to diagnose or treat any medical condition. The author and publisher are not responsible for any specific health needs that may require medical supervision and are not liable for any damages or negative consequences from any treatment, action, application, or preparation, to any person reading or following the information in this book.

References are provided for information purposes only and do not constitute endorsement of any individuals, websites, or other sources. In the event you use any of the information in this book for yourself, the author and the publisher assume no responsibility for your actions.

Books may be purchased through booksellers or by contacting Sacred Stories Publishing.

Nature: Divine Experiences with Trees, Plants, Stones and Landscapes
Ana Maria Vasquez

Tradepaper ISBN: 978-1-945026-93-5
EBook ISBN: 978-1-945026-94-2

Library of Congress Control Number: 2022931453

Published by Sacred Stories Publishing, Fort Lauderdale, FL USA

CONTENTS

PART ONE: UNDERSTANDING THE NATURAL WORLD

What is Nature? 5
How the Mystical Takes Form in Nature 7
How Nature Speaks to Us 31
Ancient Wisdom of Nature 43

PART TWO: DIVINE EXPERIENCES WITH TREES, PLANTS, STONES AND LANDSCAPES

Ruby *Ana Maria Vasquez* 51
Healing Joy *Jill Landry* 55
The Surrender *A.K. Baker* 61
Erica's Tree *Cheri Evjen* 65
The Whirl of a Leaf *Rev. Kimberly Braun* 71
The Fear Rocks *Tracy Sheppard* 75
Trees, Horses, and Transformation *Kate Neligan* 79
A Wild and Raging Storm *Anne Cederberg* 85
Tree Spirits Among Us *Dan Cavanaugh* 89
Living with a Water Spirit *Ann Marie Holmes* 93
Tim the Tree *John Paul (Eagle Heart) Fischbach* 97
Hearing Earth's Voice *Mary E. McNerney* 103
The Samauma Tree *Chris Bachmann* 107
When the Fairies Appeared *Linda Varos* 109
Grandfather Tree *Florentine Bisschops* 113
Divine Clouds *Marian S. Taylor* 117

Spirit of the Wind *Jack Allis* 121

Trinity and the Tornado *Brooke Maroldi* 125

Redwood Family and Bliss Tree *Jyoti Noel* 131

The Sacred Stones *Rev. Ariel Patricia* 135

A Life Changing Quest *Patrishe Maxwell* 139

A Tale of Two Trees *Karen B. Shea* 143

Shasta and the Platonic Solids *Tamara Knox* 147

Tree Initiation *Ysette Roces Guevara, Ph.D.* 151

Surrendering to Freedom *Dave Eyerman* 155

My Friend the Fire *Sharon M. Sirkis* 161

My Crystal Teachers *Lynne D. Chown* 165

Lift Off *Byron Edgington* 169

Sunshine and Papa Tree *Victoria Ann Glod* 175

The Medicine Wheel *Ana Maria Vasquez* 177

PART THREE: DEEPENING YOUR CONNECTION WITH NATURE

Practices to Deepen Your Nature Experiences 187

We Are Nature 205

Final Thoughts and Blessings 215

APPENDIX: BUILDING YOUR PERSONAL TREE, FLOWER, AND ROCK SYMBOLOGY LIBRARY 219

MEET OUR SACRED STORYTELLERS 227

MEET OUR FEATURED AUTHOR 233

PART ONE

Understanding the Natural World

*Forget not that the earth delights to feel your bare feet
and the winds long to play with your hair.*

— KHALIL GIBRAN

WHAT IS NATURE?

*C*ome *outside,* the natural world quietly beckons. See nature in all its wild splendor. Feel the breeze on your cheek. Smell the clean and fresh, earthy scent from the trees, the grasses, and soil. Hear the water flowing over and around the stones in the creek. Know that you are home, in the presence of an ancient ally.

Nature is a physical expression of life force energy embodied as a tree, a rock, a lake, a landscape. Some refer to life force energy as Source, Divine Intelligence, Creator, or God. I invite you to join me on this exploration of profound, mystical experiences in the natural world—you'll never look at nature the same again.

As humans, our belief in separateness has caused us to disconnect from the natural world, seeing it as a mere backdrop to our lives. Nature reminds us of a different way to move through our lives infused with rhythm and flow. There's more going on than meets the eye in the natural world. This is your invitation to uncover the wisdom that has been right in front of you all along.

The trees have told me often that humans spend a lot of time asking questions and looking for guidance, but very little time, if any, listening for

Part One

the answers. Quiet time in nature can activate this flow of inspiration that we so deeply crave and connect us to a channel of answers.

Nature has messages for us that we are energetically wired to receive—messages to help us with everyday situations. Opening us up to our highest potential, and supporting us in our expansion, nature is an easily accessible portal between the dimensions. Within these pages are some of my favorite ways to align with the natural realms and activate earth energy wisdom in our lives.

Something magical awaits each of us when we reconnect with the natural realm. Through the stories of profound personal experiences in nature shared in the pages of this book, you will remember how you can deepen your connection and understanding of the power of nature. I will also share tips and techniques to help you tune in to the messages and create an intimate relationship with the natural realm. Whether you've been a life-long nature lover or you're recently remembering the allure of the natural world, this book will evoke the curiosity and wonder that is your ticket into the mystical.

I often say, "Take it into your Listening." Instead of making an on-the-spot decision, go out in nature, sit on a rock or under a tree while looking at the landscape, and be still. As you're filled with the sights, smells, and sounds of the natural world, you're reminded of your connection to everything in the web of life. It is from this space that wisdom comes through and inspires you with new possibilities. Nature not only supports you in this endeavor, but the natural world amplifies this intention.

How would your decisions, and in turn your life, be more expanded, inspired, and on purpose if you connected with the wisdom of the natural world in a deeper way? I invite you to tune into the messages coming from nature, connecting with this ancient wisdom to remember how we can heal ourselves, and in doing that, how we can heal the planet. This is indeed Divine guidance.

HOW THE MYSTICAL TAKES FORM IN NATURE

How often have you gone to the mountains, the beach, or a park and spontaneously said, "Ah! I can breathe!" Or hiked through the woods or a wildflower field and received clarity on a life situation or a brilliant, creative idea? The wonder and mystery inherent in nature is happening all around us all the time, even though we may not see or hear it with our five physical senses. This is Mother Nature doing her magic. It is what connecting with life force energy *feels* like.

As humans, we have life force energy animating us. On top of that, we have guides, allies, and other helpers, both in physical form and in spirit. Trees, plants, stones, and landscapes embody this same energy from Source.

Because the natural realm is multidimensional, as we take our nature walk together through these chapters, we will talk about connecting with nature in two key ways. First, how we interact with the individual energetic signature of a specific tree, rose, lake, volcano, or canyon. And second, by aligning with the archetype or energetic signature guiding that plant species, landscape, or body of water. It is possible to connect on multiple levels at once.

Let's say, for example, you encounter a specific willow tree near a pond in your neighborhood. As you approach the willow and sit with your back on its trunk, you intuit the personality of this particular tree. It is refined and graceful, watching like a proud parent over the water lilies, frogs, fish, and other life forms in the pond. Turning around to look at leaves and branches, you notice some interesting protrusions on the trunk. A moment of observation reveals the shape of a human face, a male figure wearing a wizard's hat. You get the impression that the wizard is not only connecting you with this tree but also serves as the tree's guardian.

That evening, you research the archetypes of this tree species and learn that its energy represents magic, inner visions and dreams, past lessons, and maintaining emotional balance. You realize the tree's wisdom is affirming your own ability to bring grace, magic, and balance into your life and the lives of those you love.

To pay homage to all of these living energies of trees, plants, stones, and landscapes, we refer to them as beings. Stone beings. Tree beings. Plant beings. Seeing them in this way reorients us from thinking of the natural world as a backdrop, to seeing them as a crucial and participatory cast of characters we connect with while on this planet. When we bear in mind that the planet and all sentient beings on it, including us, are part of this greater life force, we begin to see the sentient nature of all things.

This doesn't mean that we are attuned to everything in the living world at all times. Given its complexity, that would be impossible. Yet, we can access pieces of this consciousness and draw on its wisdom in a way that is appropriate for us at any given time. Think about being in a shopping mall. You don't necessarily interact with every person that you see as you stroll through the mall, but you have the recognition that it's full of people. You can walk up to someone and begin a conversation if they're willing to connect with you, and they can do the same. Similarly, when you go into the forest or out in the ocean, you won't talk to every single bird, plant, mammal, rock, or sand dune that you encounter, even though you know that all these beings are there. Our curiosity, wonder, awareness, and consciousness are what activates the mystical when we are in the presence of nature.

While the natural world is so multilayered that it's practically infinite, for our purposes here, I am dividing it into the following categories.

GAIA

Throughout history, peoples and cultures around the planet have referred to the Earth as alive. The ancient Greeks named her Gaia as they looked upon her as a goddess.

Energetic aspects of Gaia include abundance, fertility, cycles, creation, nurturing, balance, harmony, beauty, and power. Gaia energy reminds us to trust and surrender to the rhythm and flow of life. She is our interconnection to all of life, reminding us of our ability to create, nurture, and bring into balance the energy within our own lives. The feminine energy of the mother runs through Gaia. As a self-contained, self-regulating system that sustains all life, she emits frequencies and harmonics that direct life on this planet.

You may think of the natural realm as what you see all around you in this glorious physical world, but it's much more than even that. Nature is a form of consciousness, the life force energy that embodies the planet. That life force begins with Gaia herself, who formed from cosmic debris made up of the elements.

These same elements comprise our bodies too. Our beautiful planet is proof that energy can neither be created nor destroyed; it simply changes form. Heat and pressure were present when our planet was forming, and that energy is still in motion, embodied through her geology and biology. We see this in the energetic lines around and through the planet.

Part One

The ancient practice of reading the land, known as geomancy, has references around the world. The idea is to have a better understanding of how the Earth herself is expressed in a particular area of land. Through this understanding, we can incorporate balance and harmony in a greater way, while harnessing earth energy naturally, thus increasing the ability for humans to connect with the unseen aspects of the natural realm and the Divine. In reading the land, various currents of energy and places where this earth energy gathers were discovered. In China, these energy lines were called "dragon lines" while other cultures referred to them as "spirit lines" or "spirit roads." Since the 1920s, they have been called "ley lines."

The way energy flows through these patterns affects our physicality as well as the land we inhabit. That is why certain places on the planet have had a propensity to emit stronger and higher vibrations than other spaces. Over time, these places became sacred sites, imprinted with the intention for mystical experiences. In this way, Gaia, the very planet herself, assists us in connecting with the magic of the natural realm.

You can sense in certain areas, particularly in wooded ones, where the convergence of energy is palpable. It's evident in the way rocks collect and congregate, how rock formations are shaped, and how moss or algae grow around them in a way that doesn't make sense. It can't be explained away through general geology. The natural energy that makes up the Earth's electromagnetic field and travels along these electrical currents collects in certain spots. Some people with high sensitivity to energy may feel these lines and power spots while others can use dowsing to determine. Those geomancers who spend large amounts of time in nature may be able to "see" these energetic lines by following the clues of the land and the natural aspects upon it. This could include lines, rows, collections of rocks that can't be explained by natural processes, and even the ways trees and plants will grow or avoid growing.

If you follow the line through, you'll notice a pattern and a pooling of energy; Nature points us to these power spaces. There are still wild spaces untouched by human beings, and if you learn how to trace energy, you can find the power spots and see how nature assembles itself in those areas. When we intuit energetic messages from the natural realm, we want to pay particular attention to anything that seems out of place or that otherwise draws our attention. This is one of the ways that the Earth reveals her power spots to us.

Our incredible planet is a living being with her own life cycle too. This phenomenon is most evident when studying the seasons—particularly at the time of the equinoxes and solstices. At these times, there is a measurable emission of frequencies that gives instructions to all of nature. It tells the trees, plants, and animals what to do and it tells us and our physical bodies what to do, because remember, we are nature too. Even though some of us may live in high-rise apartments and work in skyscrapers in the center of urban areas, a part of us receives that message. For instance, in the spring, the Earth herself wakes all of creation from its winter slumber. After many humans experience cabin fever, they feel her guidance to shake off that winter hibernation. In the summer, around the solstice, you may sense the desire to be in full expression, like the plant kingdom in its beautiful summer palette. When the autumn equinox arrives, the Earth instructs life upon her to take stock and prepare for the wintertime. Once the winter solstice arrives, the planet emits the message to go into the winter slumber, where we are all invited to slow down, go within, and dream our dream for the springtime.

Often, we think of the planet as just a big old rock and forget that appearances can be deceiving. The planet is flowing life force energy. Science can measure electromagnetic fields pulsating from the planet. Boulders, rocks, and other pieces that have broken off from the whole continue to emit these energies. As humans, we can connect with, harness, and work with these energies in a way that amplifies our intentions.

Part One

All this consciousness from Gaia flows through the trees, plants, stones, and landscapes, as well as the four directions and four elements.

TREES

Trees have witnessed generation after generation of humans come and go, so they know the human condition and understand the human energetic field. Some of them even interacted with your direct lineage. They're waiting for us to wake up and remember our alliance, our connection, our likeness to them. In terms of our energy fields and our central themes of love, compassion, and connectedness with the earth and all its inhabitants, we are more alike than we are different. The trees have this deep ancient wisdom partially because they've been here for such a long time.

Because they are amazing conduits of life force energy, it's impossible to enter the world of trees without entering the world of nature's magic. The energies of trees provide portals for you to enter, transporting you to the wisdom of the ages. Plugged into ancient universal wisdom, trees act as antennas for Divine intelligence, overflowing with messages for us about the state of our planet, as well as our inner state of being. Trees stand for truth, like sentinels standing strong and tall. The root words of "tree" and "truth" are both derived from the Old English word *treo*, meaning good faith, trust, or tree. Humans and trees have an incredible, intertwined history on both the physical and spiritual level, and now we are being called to remember this powerful alliance.

Science is making groundbreaking discoveries proving that trees communicate, have feelings, can count, and many other things no one thought possible. As advanced as our modern-day sciences are, botanists still don't completely understand miracles like how they pull water up through their root systems, turn sunlight into a sugar that feeds them, or why they give off aerosols. Although it is unclear what the aerosols do for the trees, we know that the aromatic molecular expression helps humans. While your feet crunch the pine needles on the forest floor, you enjoy that lovely scent of pine, which is basically the essential oils of the plant diffusing into the environment. These natural compounds enhance our physical, emotional, and energetic well-being. This is one reason why we feel so good in the company of trees.

Trees also emit harmonic frequencies that we can feel but are outside of our human auditory spectrum. The tree's bioenergetic field is constantly emanating energy in the form of vibrations, frequencies, and harmonics. While man-made EMFs negatively affect our bodies, these natural energies from the trees have a positive, restorative, and healing influence on us.

Specific trees provide specific support. For example, we can work with larch to release what is not needed, or fir to provide the energetic gift of seeing above and beyond. Birch is traditionally used in vision quests. One of the most amazing qualities of trees is that of generosity. From the oxygen we breathe to the fires that keep us warm, trees are true givers.

The overarching messages that come from the trees to us humans include those of deep grounding, power, resilience, transformation, wisdom, balance, and natural rhythm. When we are drawn to a particular tree, we know that those general messages are being conveyed to us, and then we can go deeper if we notice anything particular about the tree.

These are some of the symbolic qualities in general that are attributed to trees:
- Grounding
- Power
- Patience
- Transformation
- Inner magic

- Wisdom
- Natural rhythm
- Balance

Once we are aware of the general meanings of trees, we can look deeper at the species of tree and the more specific symbolic qualities attributed. This can help us hone in on the unique message a particular tree is sharing with us. In addition, the particular aspect of the tree that you are drawn to provides more interpretation for the message.

Flowers: Power and Abundance
Leaves: Wisdom and Transformation
Trunk: Healing, Strength, and Resiliency
Roots: Groundedness, Beingness, Tapping in, Connection, and Inner World

Let's say you share a frustration with a tree: Your colleagues or supervisor at work won't allow you to pursue your ideas. Then, you notice that your tree looks like it was initially growing in one direction, but something got in the way and now it's growing—and thriving—in another. It's as if the tree is saying, "Grow where you can! Send your energy to where you will be nurtured!" A sense of peace envelops you as you release a fruitless struggle. A new creative space emerges as a more helpful question dawns on you: "Where can I grow?"

Trees are perhaps the most elaborate example we have on our planet of interconnectedness. They know that they can't thrive alone. With an inherent understanding of working together holistically, either choosing to share or cut off their resources with other trees, they know it is in their best interest to work together. Regardless of species, trees help each other create a more sustainable forest. They understand that any time one of the trees is removed, for whatever reason, it creates a gap. That gap creates stress, and that stress can invite disaster for them. This is a huge and timely message to humans. We do better when we're connected to nature and to each other. We, too, need a tribe. In our modern society, we have this belief that we have to do it alone. It's an absurd concept, really, when you consider that this approach is not true anywhere else in the natural world. Without symbiosis in nature, many ecosystems would suffer and cease to flourish. That's something humans would do well to remember in our own lives.

The trees know that when we *all* do better, we all *do* better. There are mother trees in the forest that will feed trees that aren't their offspring because they know that supporting the diversity of the community is going to help the health of the entire forest.

Much like we all have totem and power animals, we also have mother trees, particular trees that support us on life's journey with wisdom, guidance, and healing. It may be an actual tree from childhood or the energy of a tree you have never physically met in this lifetime. Your personal mother tree may be revealed to you through meditation, a dream, or shamanic journeying.

What we consider mystical on some level isn't really that mystical in the world of nature—it's quite ordinary. The more we see this interchange as an everyday occurrence in our human lives, instead of a one-off, random happening, the more our lives will change in a positive direction.

We're being invited by the trees to step into a new understanding of timing, of slowing down. In fact, when you look at the science behind trees, you'll see the chemical and electrical processes are happening very, very slowly.

When we begin working with trees, we're being called into a deeper understanding of the flow of our own electrical systems, impulses, and natural rhythm which is slower and more intentional than the rhythm most of us keep on a daily basis. The importance of being in our own natural rhythm is that we're connected on a deeper level with our intuitive abilities and inner voice. Taking the cue from the trees by slowing down to find our own natural rhythm helps us better receive the guidance coming from Divine intelligence.

Trees show us how to be at peace with Divine timing. They pay attention to the cues in their environment to know whether it is time to put out their seeds or if they should hold onto them for another season. Perhaps the animal population will be down. Perhaps the bird population will be down. Both would allow their seeds a better chance at survival and propagation. They are taking chances on the weather, but all those pieces are being incorporated into the trees' inner knowing about when to put out new energy for growth. What an incredible message reflected to us in our personal lives.

Trees can imprint their wisdom on us. The sun's rays of light coming through the trees carry biophotons. Biophotons are simply light that carries information. Trees use this light by converting it to food. As the sun filters through the trees and its leaves, then onto us, we can use this energy of the biophotons to help us with our own inspirations.

You can intentionally go and sit under a tree, where you're receiving those biophotons through the leaves or the needles of the tree. While you sit there, set a strong intention about whatever you need guidance on in your life. So that you are bridging the gap between the dimensions of what's going on in your 3D reality, say your intentions in the form of your finances, relationships, connection to source, wellbeing, and health.

You can set an intention to receive guidance to learn more and expand in those areas where you're feeling constriction, so the biophotons filtering through can communicate with the light in you and imprint wisdom. It's a way of receiving the information from the tree, but also from all of life force energy that comes through the tree, the sunlight, and the atmosphere.

I have such profound gratitude to the trees for all they have shared and continue to share with me, from guidance in my daily life to taking me under their tutelage to help me better understand the profound opportunity for human and tree collaborations.

PLANTS

Plants are the superstars of the natural world. Because they sustain all of the living world, plants are the gold standard for understanding the life force energy that flows through their growth cycles. Through them, we receive nutrients, potent medicine, pure energy, and specific direction. We can connect with plants physically through gardening and walking in wild spaces, or energetically through our heart space. They are the fabric of all the landscapes and one of the key players in helping us unfold our human experiences here on the planet.

What makes plants superstars is their ability to work in synergy with their environment, transforming energy from one form to another. As alchemists of the natural world their natural compound chlorophyll enables them to absorb energy from the sun and water from their environment to photosynthesize them into food. This life-giving elixir that runs through them is used by other animals for sustenance, including humans. Alchemizing nutrients, vitamins, and minerals into forms that are easy to assimilate and thus beneficial to our human bodies, we take advantage of these vital elements that would be impossible to do on our own.

This is why when we're looking at the symbolism of plants, magic is always at the forefront. When we connect with them, we know the messages they impart will relate to the mystery in our own lives and how we are symbolically alchemizing the energy that's coming into our lives.

Plants teach us about the concept of fertility. In the spring, when plants emerge from their winter slumber and everything is in bloom, they perpetually demonstrate this attribute of potential. Those who garden know that even as we plant a tiny seed in the ground, we're already anticipating the life force contained within it. Everything that plant needs is there in the seed. What an amazing reflection to us as humans and our own seed of potential implanted in us before we incarnated here. If we can talk to the plants as our

Part One

brothers and sisters about harnessing that potential inside of us, we can use those internal resources within our individual lives to feel inspired to work in community. In doing so, we literally grow into our capacity to co-create the next dimension of heaven on earth.

Plants are extraordinarily intelligent; their physical matter and consciousness can heal the body, mind, and spirit. Serving as evolutionary guides, they show us how to awaken, grow, and live in harmony. From the vast research on plants, we know they can move their root systems toward water and turn their leaves towards the sun. Even deeper than that, a plant reacts differently when there is a human in the room versus when there is not, showing us plants' desire to interact with us.

Leading-edge technology now exists, allowing us to hear the bioenergetic field of plants. Normally, these sounds that plants are constantly emitting are outside of the audible range for humans, however, the technology translates the electrical impulses, allowing us to hear. According to the developers of this technology, at first, the plants realize that the sounds emitted by the device are a consequence of their electric activity, and then they learn to modulate it by changing the sounds. I've personally witnessed a plant mimic a vocalist note for note. Talk about a profound experience with nature!

This makes it possible for us to connect at an even deeper level with the plants, receiving their wisdom, guidance, and support through hearing their energy. This is a fun and sourcing way to calibrate your energetic field to the high vibration of nature. We already know about the potent healing qualities of plants by simply working with them on the physical level of ingesting herbs, oils, and tinctures. When we couple this herbalist knowledge with the cutting-edge technology that delivers the audible harmonics of a plant, we begin working with the plants in an interdimensional way. And still, we've barely scratched the surface of our collaboration with plants.

Plants are woven into the fabric of our lives through landscapes, gardens, and greenery in our homes, but also through the ways they serve us as a food source and medicine, both pharmaceutical—over a quarter of synthetic medicines are derived from plants—as well as natural medicines of herbs, oils, and plant tinctures that balance our physical bodies. In addition to the physical effects, herbs, plant material, and essential oils help us raise our vibration. Be sure that you activate that plant material through gratitude and intention to work with it in a new way, instead of just using the plants. Another way is to really infuse yourself with the music that comes from the biofield of the plants or the trees, working especially with the music of those plants that have the energetic resonance you're looking to bring into your life. For example, if you're looking to bring more magic into your life, the music of a cedar tree would be helpful in harnessing the energy of magic.

STONES

Stones have ancient, galactic imprinting on them. As the universe was formed, a tremendous amount of heat was created. As it cooled over millions of years, this planetary dust came together as planets, moons, and stars. On our planet, as volcanoes erupted, flowing molten lava to form the land, igneous rocks like basalt and granite formed as they were exposed to the elements of wind, water, and sunlight. As this foundational rock became broken down and scattered about, it settled on fjords, beach floors, riverbeds, lakes, and up against the valley floors. Over time, as this rock layered upon itself, it formed sedimentary rock such as shale, sandstone, and limestone. From more of that intense pressure, they shifted and changed into metamorphic rocks like marble.

Rocks, like other living beings, are in a constant state of change with their own style of life cycles. Stones may look static, but they are constantly emitting their own high-frequency vibrations that can be measured at regular intervals. We are affected by this when we come in contact with them, se pulses of frequency can help elevate our vibration. By adding our ins, we can piggyback onto that energy, amplifying those intentions. The rocks are naturally affecting the subtle energy field, making this a potent space for you to set or recommit to an intention that you have.

We can draw on inherent attributes of stones for use in our own lives. By tuning into their energy, we can learn the virtues of patience, strength, acceptance, stability, integrity, adaptability to change, holding various perspectives, and the ability to withstand anything that comes our way while surrendering to Divine flow.

Certain stones are fantastic conductors and amplifiers of energy that can both hold and transmit vibration. This is why our modern-day electronics are made with quartz and silica. Actual data can be imprinted onto them, and they can resonate out that frequency. For example, quartz is recognized for its technological ability to amplify energy, and is currently used in our computers, cell phones, lasers, etc. Similarly, the quartz and silica elements of rocks can serve as conduits for amplifying our own frequencies and intentions. You don't have to recreate Stonehenge to have this interaction. You can recreate that intention just by sitting on or with a rock.

As there is such potent energy available to us from stone beings, the first step is to change your perspective of the cliff faces, boulders, rocks, stones, and pebbles from simply being backdrops in nature. As we consciously connect more and understand the process that rocks undergo in their perpetual evolution it allows us to collaborate more intentionally with the stone beings. This helps us choose which stones may be the best collaborators for specific needs.

Instinctually, you have probably experienced this power from rocks and stones. Have you ever felt drawn to carry a stone in your pocket or hold it in your hand when you feel stressed? Are you always finding and picking up pebbles or pieces of rock when you're out in nature? Pay attention to what type of stone you are drawn to and study its characteristics. Notice the information coming through your clairsenses as you connect with the rocks.

The more we collaborate with the stone beings, the more we begin to synchronize our energy fields with rocks, allowing us to harness the subtle energies to amplify our manifestations. The stone beings teach us about transformation and reincarnation, as their life cycle embodies these processes. Our ancestors built stone circles and stone temples to harness the energetic qualities of rocks to assist in their own spiritual connection and transformation.

LANDSCAPES

Landscapes are made up of rocks, plants, animals, microorganisms, and systems that give off a particular energy. It's important to understand the individual energies coming through them, as it varies from one landscape to another. For instance, the energy present on the bank of a river differs from the energy in a desert. Any landscape that we work with teaches us about adaptability.

When I lived in Crestone, Colorado, I wanted to understand what was going on there geologically and why it's known as a place that contains a massive creative vortex. I learned that it's a place where the Earth's crust is opening and new crust is being formed, essentially creating new earth. There are huge quartz crystal fields, all with the sacred geometry of nature embedded, that further amplify these natural energies. Additionally, people who work on anchoring in that energy of expansion while connected with intention, open it up even more. Living in that landscape, I personally experienced a major shift and expansion in my inner work and my professional endeavors.

Landscapes help us reflect on our inner landscape. Traveling, of course, is a good time to engage with landscapes. As you encounter them in your car, on a train, or by flying over them in a plane, pay attention to how you feel when you see them, the emotions that come up, and the thoughts that they trigger. If you're hiking through a rain forest or a tropical location, it's easy to feel peace and bliss. At the opposite end of the emotional spectrum, traveling through an area that has been ravaged by a tornado, fires, or flooding may bring up feelings of anger, despair, hopelessness, or personal devastation. Allow the land to help you process these emotions as you simultaneously send high vibrations and love to source them in their recovery. The stronger the element of the landscape and what it evokes within you, plus the longer you are in contact with that landscape, equates to a greater energy exchange between you and the landscape. This results in a greater effect on the land, as well as within us, allowing for greater transformation.

In addition to the overall energetic attribute of adaptability, certain types of landscapes carry with them specific characteristics. Here are a few:

- **Beaches and oceans:** The energy of healing. Shorelines are doorways to the spiritual realm. Where the element of earth meets the element of water, it creates a potent energetic space known for creating a mental shift. The vastness of these spaces helps to channel infinite wisdom. These are powerful spaces for ceremony and connecting with ancestors.
- **City landscapes:** These speak to the importance of having a solid foundation in your own life. They reflect community, diversity, and synergy. Pay attention to the unity and cohesiveness, as well as what is fractured. What are the social issues going on and how does it affect the landscape? Cities are complex systems with many moving parts and a fast pace. You can work with city energy to harness those big waves of energy to support your intentions and manifestations.

City landscapes can help you see where you are in synergy in your own life and where you are making things harder for yourself.

- **Deserts:** These arid environments are all about creativity, adaptability, and how it is used for our very survival. Due to its vastness, deserts are powerful in terms of spiritual revelations. Deserts have quite a diverse ecosystem, reminding us that there is more going on than meets the eye, which beckons us deeper into our spiritual quests.
- **Lakes and ponds:** These bring the energy of a soothing oasis of relaxation and energetic nourishment. These bodies of water symbolize our consciousness. Is the water still or troubled? Are you taking a deep dive or are you staying near the surface? An entire ecosystem exists below the surface.
- **Rivers and creeks:** The flow of life is on display with these water features in nature. Wildness and a reflection of our emotions. The ability to navigate obstacles in our life with ease and grace. Where in your life are you experiencing flow and where does it feel like there's a dam?
- **Meadows and fields:** These represent slow, steady growth and the balance of life. Joy, growth, expansion, space, and interconnectedness. Spending some time in stillness in a meadow may assist you in calling in the inspiration for the unfolding of your purpose work.
- **Forests:** Here we have the primal, feminine energies represented, along with unrestricted growth and our unconscious mind. Mystery, magic, symbiosis, abundance, wildness. A forest walk is an ideal way to invoke the magic and wonder of a new phase in your life, to offer up some fertile ground in which your dreams can take root.
- **Mountains:** These represent our own spiritual power to overcome obstacles, reaching our highest peaks and pinnacles. The power and majesty of a mountain is awe-inspiring. Mountain tops are another doorway to the spiritual realm. A powerful space where the element

of earth meets the element of air. The magnitude of the energy of the earth is on full display, allowing us to interact with that potent life force energy. Mountains throughout time have been home to the gods. Communing with a mountain is to interact with something much, much bigger than yourself, giving perspective and reminding you of the bigger picture.

THE ELEMENTS

The ancients believed that the world is comprised of four basic elements that sustain life: water, air, fire, and earth. These essential energy forces combined to create life with assistance from a fifth element—that of ether, or spirit. They are not only integral components of the material universe, but also elements that exist within all humans. This is why working with these four elements is powerful and influential for us. By connecting with them and understanding their presence within us, we become aware of our connection with nature and our relationship with the Divine. Connecting with and honoring the four elements allows us to honor and understand ourselves and our link to the world around us in a more insightful way.

Water can be found in oceans, seas, lakes, rivers, and springs, both above and underground. Life on our beautiful planet would not be possible without water, as every living creature from microorganisms to mammals depends on it. Our human bodies are composed of more than three quarters water.

It's no surprise that this element represents flow, calm, and clarity. Its transformative nature makes it a cleanser and purifier. We may ask ourselves where are we in the flow in our lives and where are we stagnant? Water also has a link to our emotions. Where are we overwhelmed by our emotions? Where have we turned our emotions off?

It is symbolic of dreaming, healing, fluidity, purification, regeneration, stability, strength, change, fertility, devotion, receiving, and unconditional love. It symbolizes death as well as rebirth. It is life-giving but can also be destructive.

Fresh water stands for life and good health, while polluted or stagnant water is symbolic of bad health. It is associated with the autumn season and the west direction.

Air can be found all around us, but its most visible manifestation is through breezes or winds. Like water, air is the element of life itself as all living creatures, both plants and animals, require it to live and thrive. It is what fills our lungs and every cell of our bodies.

It is associated with the breath of life and attributed to transcending power. Air symbolizes communication, intelligence, perception, knowledge, learning, thinking, imagination, creativity, harmony, and travel. The element of air helps us transcend our lower thinking mind and connect with Divine intelligence. This source of life can also, at times, become a force of terrible destruction. We can call on the element of air when we need the winds of change in our lives. Air is associated with the spring season and the east direction.

Fire was the first element to be created when the universe was born. It gives off light, and is transformative, and when merged with other elements, it can change and grow. For instance, when fire encounters air, it grows bigger and burns brighter.

Fire is reflected in our blood and our body temperature. It speaks to the power of transmutation, burning away everything and leaving only truth to grow from the ashes. It also corresponds to being in full expression, much like a large bonfire.

Part One

Fire is attributed to transformational and purifying powers. It can give warmth and enable life, and it can also burn and destroy. In the spiritual plane, fire stands for Light. The element symbolizes incredible energy, activity, creativity, passion, freedom, power, love, vision, anger, strength, will, assertiveness, courage, dynamism, desire, and passion. When I need clarity about a particular situation in my life, I like to work with the element of fire to burn away anything that is not my truth. It is associated with the summer season and the south direction.

The **Earth** element can be found in fields, hills, mountains, and plains, and is home to all living beings. Survival would be impossible without earth. Its fertility provides energy and sustenance to all living creatures.

Our bodies are composed of minerals of the earth in the form of our bones. It allows us to complete the energetic circuit in our connection, amplifying and magnifying our intentions. Earth reminds us to ground deeply here in this physical reality to connect to Divine wisdom.

It symbolizes prosperity, fertility, stability, orderliness, groundedness, sustenance, creativity, physical abundance, nourishment, solidity, dependability, security, permanence, intuition, introspection, and wisdom.

We can connect with the element of earth when we are looking to better embody and apply spiritual principles in our lives. It is associated with the winter season and the north direction. The ancestors are also associated with the element of earth.

ELEMENTALS

When we contemplate the spirit of a tree, rock, mountain, or lake, those energies have a physical component that we can see. The realm of the elementals, by contrast, is where nature's dazzling magic transcends the physical and becomes truly multidimensional, as these beings are composed of etheric matter.

What does this charmed, subtle realm consist of? Each tree, flower, plant, stone, and landscape have a nature spirit associated with it. This is different from the spirit of a plant or tree. The easiest way to understand nature spirits is to think of them as being similar to spirit guides, who assist in maintaining harmony and balance within the natural world. Elementals are like the caretakers who look after trees, plants, and landscapes. When you see a figure or face in a tree, stone, or elsewhere in the natural world, you are catching a glimpse of the nature spirit associated with that natural aspect. In the invisible realm, consider the difference between a small pinecone seed and a massive pine tree. The elementals are the intelligent sparks of consciousness who work with the energy of the seed, helping it grow into a strong, towering tree.

These nature spirits are called elementals because they are typically associated with the elements of air, fire, water, and earth. For example, the element of:

Earth includes gnomes, brownies, dryads, pans, elves, and more. These elementals work with the soil, rocks, and roots. Besides helping humans connect with earth energies, they assist us with our physical bodies and physical senses.

Water includes the undines, water sprites, mermaids, naiads, and others. These elementals watch over the planet's water, be it a lake, river, marsh, or ocean. They help us connect with these water features and assist us in working with the watery aspects of our emotions.

Part One

Air includes the sylphs. Their domain is the air, clouds, and wind. These elementals assist us with inspiration, getting out of our heads, and obtaining mental clarity. They can help us engage with life force energy through the breath.

Fire includes the elementals known as salamanders, which shares no relation to the amphibian known as the salamander. They get their name from the lizard-like shapes that can often be seen in the flames of a fire. In ancient times, it was believed that the amphibian itself was born from the fire because when old logs were thrown onto a fire, they would scurry out of the flames. Salamanders can source us when we are going through a life transformation or need to be in fuller self-expression.

When researching and working with the elementals, you may come across the term "deva." Devas are largely considered the overseers of the elementals, much like archangels in relation to the angelic realm. Devas are the metaphysical forces behind nature that support the earth's ecology. When we use the phrase "forces of nature," we are essentially referring to the powerful traits of these entities.

Fairies also have a special place in the realm of the elementals. While they are steeped in myth and folklore, physics justifies that these beings, in the form of electromagnetic matter, do exist in the subtle realm. Fairies are commonly associated with flowers, plants, animals, and insects. You can call on the fairies to help grow and nurture the plants in your home and garden. They have been known to help humans with uninvited animals, critters, and insects. For instance, if you have a mouse in your pantry, call on the fairies to help escort the creature to a more appropriate location.

As with all the natural aspects, some people are more predisposed to connect with the elementals than others. Some can see them physically while others recognize that elementals are present by seeing unexplained tiny

Understanding the Natural World

colored lights, especially in their peripheral vision, or evening hearing tiny bells. Others encounter these nature spirits through their intuitive channels, like the ability to hear them in their mind's ear.

Caring for the natural world and a sincere intention to connect deeply with nature is one of the best ways to attract and connect with the elementals. You can also create an inviting and hospitable environment for them by putting out a fairy house, shiny trinkets, fruits, and sweets. Placing small statues or likenesses of elementals, like garden gnomes, lets them know they are welcome.

The trees, rocks, plants, and landscapes do convey messages to us. The key is to expect the possibility of having an interaction with them that is intelligent and profound. The more that we consciously put ourselves in situations with nature, the more these mystical experiences happen. I've found that they most often occur when we're at a pivotal transition point in life, or in a place of surrender where we're able to say, "I don't know what's going to happen. I don't know what to do. I don't have any more answers. I've done everything I can and now I'm open to the Divine coming through in any way—be it through the wisdom of a tree, an animal, an angel, or an element such as fire or wind."

Do you need to believe in the mystical aspect of nature to have magical experiences? Not at all. The life force energy that moves through all of creation is so powerful it doesn't need you to believe in it. Personally, if I'm not seeing magic and awe in my life, I know that it's time to get out in nature. I realize that I'm not going to create anything profound in my life or be able to share anything truly meaningful with others if I'm creating from a space of stagnancy that is devoid of life force. None of us can, really. Thank goodness that we can partner with nature to release, be sourced, and return to our vibrant selves.

Part One

Nature serves as a portal to the interdimensional realms of universal intelligence. As we connect to our heart space through our admiration, curiosity, and wonder of the natural realm, our breath naturally slows and deepens, activating our heart coherence. This heart coherence serves as a bridge to the quantum field, our source for infinite possibilities. Nature serves as a conduit to our human development and expansion.

As a physical embodiment of life force energy, nature can serve as a tangible representation with which we can connect to those unseen, interdimensional, high-vibrational allies for insight, wisdom, healing, guidance, inspiration, protection, and more. This allows for a deeper connection to the Divine through nature.

The natural world is phenomenal. We have a synergistic relationship with nature for our physical bodies through food, nutrients, medicine, fuel, and a vast assortment of materials. Beyond the physical, we have real allies in the natural realm.

Each human embodied on this planet makes an impact in the ecology around them throughout their lifetime. Humans are also infinite beings embodied in the physical with access to these infinite realms and extrasensory perceptions. The same is true for the beings in the natural realm. They have a physical aspect and role that they play in the circle of life, and they also have access to the unseen realms and energy. We all share this planet, this ecology—we're all in it together—so it behooves us to connect on all levels, seen and unseen, to create a better world for all of us.

HOW NATURE SPEAKS TO US

"We still do not know one thousandth of one percent of what nature has revealed to us." Albert Einstein said this in the early 20th century, and it still holds true today. This is why I find it so joyful to explore, experiment with, and play with the natural world. The revelations and creations are infinite!

While it might be easy to understand what your dog or cat is conveying through barks, meows, and scratching on the screen door, it may be more of a reach to consider that the wind responds to our emotions, crystals can imbue us with confidence, or water can read our thoughts. That's the beauty of it. We don't hold an expectation that a flower or mountain is going to open its mouth and speak, so we can immediately expand our perception of all the possible ways that these sentient beings can relate to us. It is more likely that nature will speak to you through symbology, synchronicities, and archetypes, all of which can evoke powerful emotions and take on a profound significance for each person.

Establishing a dialogue with the wonderful world of nature begins with simply having an admiration for or curiosity about something, then allowing yourself to become exquisitely attentive and aware. For instance, you may feel attracted to a photo of a lush rain forest or in awe of the majestic landscape before you while atop the mesa you've just hiked. Staring at the perfection of a rose bud or river rock endears you to this living object in a way that begins to create a resonance.

With your heart center now activated, you start to feel gratitude for the beauty that is now captivating you. At this point, your interaction with nature becomes more than just physical. It begins to create frequencies that are emitted from your energy field, causing it to further expand. As your vibration rises, you may even experience feelings of love and compassion emanating from you to that rain forest, rosebud, landscape, or river rock.

Holding that higher frequency, you might start to sense that love or other qualities are being transmitted to you from this nature being. Keeping your intuitive channel in a receptive mode gives space for this two-way dialogue to happen, though on a different level than you may be accustomed to at first. How this occurs is going to depend on how you're wired. Just as most of us have one or two dominant physical senses, we also have dominant intuitive senses, and we all connect with Spirit in our own unique ways. Is the energy something you're seeing in your mind's eye or in the physical? Is it something you're hearing in your mind's ear or audibly that's underscoring a question you've just asked? Is it an emotion, physical sensation, or a knowing that just drops in?

Questions are a great way to begin your dialogue with nature. Ask the tree or plant if it has any insights into a situation you're struggling with or inquire about its own experience—for instance, *What's it like to be a tree?* Then wait for the answers. Sometimes, words may appear in your mind that aren't typically what you'd come up with on your own. Other times, a quiet awareness or idea will arise. Or your attention might be drawn to a particular feature of the tree.

Similar to the turn of the seasons, the development of your intuition is cyclical. Once you become comfortable with establishing this back-and-forth conversation, you can begin to work on intentionally connecting with any aspect of nature. The more time you spend doing this, the more you will experience greater connection, expansion, and oneness. This may happen for you all at once or you may feel the process unfold over the course of time. For most, it's not a linear journey, but rather like the spirals that can be found everywhere in the natural world, from whirlpools and hurricanes to the concentric rings on the trunk of an ancient redwood—ever growing as you grow.

You will be using your five senses just like you do in your day-to-day life, as well as adding onto it your innate extrasensory capacities, described below. This is the true meeting point between you and the trees, stones, plants, and landscapes.

CLAIRVOYANCE

Clairvoyance, or clear seeing, is the ability to receive intuitive impressions through images, flashes of pictures, colors, or shapes in your peripheral or inner vision. If you are a visual person, like an artist, designer, or builder, clairvoyance is most likely a dominant sense for you. With this capability, you are combining your physical sight with your ability to see with your energetic eyes. Clairvoyant visions can relate to the past, present, or future.

When you first begin experimenting with this sense, you may get only glimpses of visuals. As you progress, this type of sight may become much more detailed, like watching scenes from a movie. I have found that the way in which we experience seeing memories in our mind's eye is how we will typically receive intuitive impressions through clairvoyance. For example, think back to a time you spent out in nature. The way that you see that

Part One

memory in your mind is how you can see or receive messages through your clairvoyant channel.

In addition to intuitive messages that come through your clairvoyant channel, you can, of course, see pieces of intuitive information with your physical eyes. You may begin to notice and see plants, rocks, or something that looks out of place or grabs your attention; these images may invoke messages or emotions that are personal to you. For instance, a particular rock outcropping catches your eye because you see on it the perfectly formed shape of a howling wolf. You feel that this wolf, through the rock, is urging you to stand firmly grounded in your power and speak your truth without fear of reprisal. While walking along the shore and watching a glorious sunrise in the east, you are reminded of all the possibilities and opportunities that this new day holds for you, and to be in the flow and current of life.

CLAIRAUDIENCE

Clairaudience, or clear hearing, is the ability to receive intuitive impressions through words inside of your mind or by sounds, words, or music that you hear outside of your mind that is relevant to the question you're asking. It may not actually be audible, but an impression of the word on your mind. Those whose talents lie in our auditory faculties, like gifted musicians, singers, writers, and public speakers probably have clairaudience as a leading sense.

Clairaudience usually comes in short, concise bits of information, and as you listen, you can track it bit by bit to form a longer narrative. The words may or may not sound like your thinking voice. For example, look at your grocery list. As you go through the list in your head, hear yourself saying each item as if you are speaking aloud. Similarly, messages from nature may come through your clairaudient channel and sound like your thinking voice. Other times, when you're connecting with nature, you may hear a voice in your head that doesn't sound like yours; what you may be hearing is the energy coming from nature. Either way, you're on the right track if the information coming through pertains to the question you have on your mind and is of a vibration of love not fear.

Another way that nature can speak to you through your clairaudience is when you hear an actual nature sound, like wind rustling through leaves, an echo around the mountain, or the crackling sound of a fire. It may spark a remembrance within you from childhood or remind you that the winds of change are approaching and to set your intentions, so you are sourced by these changes, rather than being blown around and disturbed by them.

CLAIRSENTIENCE

Clairsentience, or clear feeling, allows us to receive messages in the form of feelings, emotions, or other physical sensations. The focus with this sense is on the physical and emotional body. Many of us are clairsentient without consciously being aware of it. When we get a strong gut feeling about someone we've just met or when we get the chills for no apparent reason, we may be tuning into the emotional energy of a person or a spirit around us.

Some of us are empaths. We are highly sensitive and in tune with not only our own feelings, but those of others, including the beings in the natural world. Empaths are natural healers and can be found carrying out their soul missions as doctors, therapists, educators, and caregivers of all kinds.

When you receive a message through your clairsentience, you might feel uncertain about where the emotion is coming from and what it means. You might get stuck in your head instead of being in your heart. The element of water is a great sourcing ally in these cases. Call on it to help you stay in the flow and allow more fluid insights to come through. You may even want to drink a big glass of water to help the information come through with greater ease.

Plants are genius at sending signals through clairsentience. You might get tingling sensations, phantom sensations in your body, or feel overwhelmed in a good way when near a particular plant. Let's say you're walking in nature with the intention of being open to its wisdom when you come across a mulberry bush. Stopping to observe this fruity shrub, you notice feelings of sweetness arising from within your heart center. As you connect in with this sensation, a profound sense of deep acceptance about who you are is directed at you from the bush. In your gut, you know that this plant is prompting you to be aware of your interconnection to the whole, and how much you are loved and supported. For the rest of the weekend, you carry that feeling with you, allowing it to support you.

CLAIRCOGNIZANCE

We experience claircognizance, or clear knowing, when we become aware of insights, wisdom, inspired ideas, and even solutions. This is when we have knowledge of people or events that we would not normally have knowledge about. Many philosophers, professors, doctors, scientists, religious leaders, and business innovators have strong claircognizance. This potent way of receiving intuitive information is the least likely of the clairsenses to be misinterpreted but most likely to be dismissed because the information simply drops in.

Spirit impresses us with truths that pop into our minds from out of nowhere, like a premonition about something that will happen in the future. With this extra sense, seeing is not believing—believing is seeing! The knowingness shows up first, followed by confirmation from the physical world. While eating your breakfast, you suddenly have a knowingness that abundance is about to come into your life. The next day while on a road trip, you get visual confirmation as you drive by farmers on their combines reaping their copious harvests and you experience the same knowingness of abundance like you did the morning before. You feel in your solar plexus that good things are about to happen, and they soon do.

When working with your claircognizant abilities, it's important to go with the initial impression you receive and resist dropping into your analytical mind to figure it out. When an intuitive knowing comes to you, consciously take a few deep, full breaths. This intentional use of the element of air can bring you back to a heart space to receive more guidance.

CLAIRALIENCE AND CLAIRGUSTANCE

Clairalience, or clear smelling, is being able to smell odors that don't have any kind of physical source. The scent of peonies may be present, reminding you that a deceased loved one is around in spirit. Certain smells can connect you to memories, like traces of briny ocean air wafting through your meditation space during your morning practice. Often accompanying clairalience, clairgustance, or clear tasting, is the ability to taste something that isn't there. You might experience the aroma of a pine forest and, at the same time, have a distinct taste in your mouth.

While doing a private client session in my office, I experienced the distinct smell of campfire smoke as she spoke about what was going on in her life. Immediately, I knew it was a message from nature about how she had lost her spark and passion for life. "I'm just going through the motions," she shared with me when I relayed this knowing. "I feel like I'm getting battered every day by a barrage of criticism at work and in my marriage," she continued.

As I tuned in to ask her allies from the natural realm for more guidance, they suggested that she spend some time with the element of fire—if not by being near a fireplace or campfire, then simply by sitting with a candle. My client went on to do this, and it served to reactivate the fire within her, enabling her to speak up for herself and make some crucial shifts to bring more balance and harmony into her life.

DREAM TIME

I would be remiss to not mention our dream state as a way in which nature speaks through the astral realm. We receive so much information this way because when the conscious mind is asleep, the subconscious mind has space to speak. The same parameters apply as with the above senses, only in these situations, the messages are conveyed through our dreams, even if we don't remember them.

Consider doing a simple ritual during the potent moments before going to sleep. Engage the life force of air by taking a few deep breaths and drop into the heart space. Once you feel centered, ask a question. If you are new to this process, start with a question that has a simple "yes" or "no" answer—for instance, *Should I proceed with the new career opportunity that has been presented to me?* Or *Am I on the right track to resolving this issue around my health?* Upon waking, even if you have no recollection of your dream, take a few deep breaths, and ask your question again. Trust that your subconscious was indeed interacting with the quantum field while you were sleeping. When you ask the question, observe how you feel. Do you feel heavy or light? Anxious or calm? This alone can provide a wealth of information. Sensations of heaviness or anxiety may indicate a "no" or "not now" response to your inquiry, whereas, if you feel an elevation in your energy, this could be your green light to proceed.

Let's say you have a dream you go on a road trip to the deserts of the Southwest. While exploring these vast, arid lands, you come across a patch of vibrant, thriving green plants with colorful blooms. As you inspect them up close, admiring their beauty and fragrance, a rattlesnake suddenly strikes at you from behind a grouping of stones. Barely missing his bite, you wake up in a panic. As you regain your composure through a few minutes of rhythmic breathing, insights begin to come through. You've been feeling a little lost lately, like you're wandering in a vast desert with no direction. The thriving plant life reminds you that there is more to life than how you are currently living and that it's important to slow down and savor the beauty of each day. You instinctually know that rattlesnake represents the anxiety you've been experiencing because of listening to the strong opinions of others telling you what you should do. The guidance from the natural realm is clear: You need to release the opinions of people in your life who are not serving your wellbeing and personal growth.

How can you begin to experiment with all these senses in nature? It can be as simple as sitting near a river or in your garden. Go where you feel led. If you feel centered while sitting in your garden or your worries seem to fade into the background when you're snowshoeing through a fresh snowfall, then lean into those propensities. Follow what lights you up. If a certain natural space brings you a sense of inner peace and well-being, you are innately opening yourself to the messages that are ready to come through from the intelligent natural world. You might find one plant or landscape that stands out amongst all the others, or a specific color or shape of a rock or flower that draws you in. Again, think about how we interact with other human beings. We're drawn to some and not others for different reasons and we can't explain why. The same thing applies with the natural world. These beings just look differently than we do.

For those living in more urban settings without easy access to nature, consider that you're being led to work more energetically than physically. Work with photographs or other depictions of a tree, beach, or mountain, or invoke a memory from when you spent time outdoors. Take advantage of local parks, botanical gardens, or walking trails if they are accessible. Volunteer at your community garden or CSA. Bring nature indoors with house plants by creating a windowsill herb garden. Just putting your fingers in the dirt and coming in contact with its microbial wonders can be enough to establish a connection. Even just stepping outside and breathing the air can help you stay connected as high-vibrational frequencies are constantly being broadcast from the natural world.

TIPS FOR CONNECTING NATURALLY

- **Let go of any expectation.** Your communication with nature does not have to look or feel a certain way. It doesn't have to arrive as a booming voice or mystical vision. More often than not, nature speaks to us in the form of a gentle luring. How messages come through will be highly personal to you.
- **Create your own symbology library.** Your own interpretation of what the messages from nature mean to you is important. For this reason, I invite you to cultivate your own personal nature symbology library. To do this, ask yourself what comes to mind when you think of various aspects of the natural world, like a mountain, lake, or tulip. Keep a list of these personal meanings and refer to them as needed.
- **Follow your wonder and curiosity.** Allow nature to feed you cues that are most relevant and appropriate for you and remain open to whatever they may be. Bear in mind that everything has a purpose for showing up in your experience and catching your attention.
- **Notice how you feel.** As you listen for nature's voice and follow the cues, pay attention to how these inklings of information sit in your physical and emotional body. Do they feel heavy or light?

The message may not be what you expected or wanted, but does it resonate? Any messages from the Divine intelligence of the natural realm will be of a high vibration based in love, not fear.

- **Practice, practice, practice!** Like any relationship, what you put into it is what you get out of it. Take time on a consistent basis to nurture your connection to nature, even if it's just a few minutes a day observing the oak tree through the window in your front yard.
- **Honor your alliance with nature.** Show up authentically and with reverence. Think of yourself as a guardian and supporter of nature in return for its protection and support.

I encourage you to have fun exploring all these senses while realizing they can be transformational in your life. Your relationship with nature can be quite profound because the natural world acts as a mirror for your inner terrain. It will illuminate for you what's going on both on an individual and collective level.

Through its wisdom and power, you can come to understand your own wild nature and how to thrive to the fullest. You can remember your own natural rhythm and flow and apply it to your life for more peace and harmony. The more you allow trees, plants, stones, and landscapes to serve as your portal to Divine communication, the more seamlessly you will move through the world with a heightened awareness that sources, soothes, and heals you and the planet.

ANCIENT WISDOM OF NATURE

Interconnection, reverence, respect, responsibility, and reciprocity. Never taking without giving back. Around the globe, ancient and modern indigenous wisdom shares the ideal of being a guardian and protector of the Earth. The idea is reflected in the Maori word *kaitiakitanga*, which means guarding and protecting the environment to respect the ancestors and secure the future.

Our ancient ancestors deeply understood the connection between the Earth and themselves. They had an understanding that whatever was happening to the natural world was a reflection of what was happening to the humans. There was an absolute belief that nature and the Earth herself was indeed a living entity and it shaped the way they did things in everyday life. They had an intimate relationship and were immersed in nature and the elements. They observed, studied, and did ceremonies around the seasons, the cycle of the moon, the elements, and the animals to maintain harmony with the natural world. Because their survival depended on this relationship, they had to be tuned in to any changes in the environment or energy field.

The attention they paid to the world around them also extended to the energetic realm, the unseen energies. Shamanic journeying, dreams, and medicinal plants provided insight and guidance to individuals and the collective.

Increasingly, modern science is turning to the knowledge and wisdom of indigenous peoples to help make sense of data gathered and create a more holistic view about the Earth and her bionetwork. It is in this sweet spot where science meets spirituality that true understanding, collaboration, and expansion takes place. The weaving of the two intelligences can only enhance our understanding of the world around us.

If you observe nature, you will see how the elements that form its basis can help balance each other. Water mitigates fire and air moderates fire, modeling for us how to balance opposing forces within ourselves and in the world around us. The ancient people understood the delicate balance taking place in nature by being mindful in how and when they took things from the natural world. It was customary to ask the natural world for permission before modifying it in any way, be it through harvesting crops, gathering flowers, or killing an animal. Their respect was so great that cautionary tales of what can happen if you don't show that respect became a part of their origin stories.

Being in harmony with our environment is a primal, foundational requirement of our human experience. Our ancestors understood the power of the natural realm, and they worked with it intentionally. The more they did this and the deeper their relationship with nature was, the more they learned about the unseen world. That's one of the reasons why they took on tasks like assembling stone circles and temples. Because they intensely studied and deeply connected with the natural elements, they knew that each rock held its own vibration that could support the purpose of a particular stone circle or structure. Assembling stones in specific ways could either shield or amplify the frequencies of that particular land area and the harmonics of the stones being used. Aligning with these electromagnetic fields enabled them to receive profound insights about their everyday lives, including the changes occurring and the mystical knowledge they wouldn't have been able to receive on their own.

Ancestral wisdom that was imprinted into the rocks, trees, and landscapes all over the planet is available to us today. As we connect and deeply listen, we have access to that knowledge, wisdom, and guidance to apply to our present lives. Be attentive. Listen deeply to the natural realm.

I'm honored to be sharing my mystical experiences with nature alongside our sacred storytellers. While each of them is beautifully expressed by the individual authors, I also see Part Two as the storytelling of Nature herself.

PART TWO

Divine Experiences with Trees, Plants, Stones and Landscapes

Everything in nature invites us constantly to be what we are.

—GRETEL EHRLICH

RUBY

"Well, let's see what happens." I leaned into the tree and placed my bare hands on its sturdy trunk.

Immediately feeling self-conscious, I took a few minutes to center myself, clear my mind, and tune into the tree's wisdom. I had everything to gain by trying this and nothing left to lose. In a span of 18 months, my life had completely fallen apart. I'd lost my job, my home, my relationship, and one of my soul dogs, and moved back home with my dad.

At the height of this low point, amidst the rubble of my former life, I decided to embark on a quest to discover the viability of the spiritual principles I'd been exploring for several years. *This is where the rubber meets the road,* I reasoned. *Now is my opportunity to put my spiritual practices into action so I can survive this life tsunami.* From that point forward, I began to take everything I'd been studying about the energetics of animals and the natural world, something I'd always had a strong connection to, and turn it into my living laboratory.

For as long as I could remember, my deepest desire was to be able to communicate with animals telepathically. If I had to rebuild my life anyway, then I wanted to do so in a more authentic and connected way. Intuitively, I knew that remembering my connection to all sentient beings was part of this process of embodiment. My spiritual teachers reassured me that everyone has an inherent ability to communicate with animals and nature.

"Your openness to recalibrating your energy field to that of the natural world and allowing it to raise your frequency will determine your capacity to connect with animals and receive their messages," they instructed.

With the hope that they were right, that I really could communicate with the animal world, I mustered the courage to do a simple assignment they'd given me: Connect with a tree through my sense of touch, and do this practice every day for a month.

So, here I was, with my hands on the trunk. I began to talk to it, like I would a person.

"Okay, tree, I'm not sure I'm doing this technique right, or if I'm even touching you in an inappropriate place," I nervously overexplained. "To be honest, I have a lot of fear that this won't work for me. If it doesn't, then what will I be left with? I so want to step into a more spiritually conscious life! If you can please take the small speck of faith that I have in this process and amplify it, I would be so grateful."

Nothing in particular or special seemed to be happening as I spoke these words, nor when I did this same process for the next few weeks. Despite my doubts, I visited the tree every day, placed my hands on the trunk, and spoke to it with whatever was on my mind and in my heart.

Somewhere around the third week, while sitting in my living room in contemplation, I asked myself a question. As soon as I spoke the words out loud, I heard a verbal response that seemed to be coming from outside in the yard. A mixture of shock and joy pulsed through my body, as I realized the answer was being sent to me from the same tree I had been interacting with every day. From right there in the living room, I continued this extraordinary exchange with the tree.

"Was that you?" I asked it.

Yes, the tree responded, quite simply and clearly.

"How is that even *possible?*"

No response.

"Well, if that *was* you, then tell me . . . what's your name?"

I instantly felt the name Ruby.

"Ruby. Is that right?"

I felt a yes.

Elated that I was now in actual communication with the tree, the next question flew out of my mouth before I had time to censor it.

"I don't want to sound ungrateful, but my desire is to talk to the animals. I'm in awe that you are communicating with me, but I'm not sure what to do with a talking tree*!* I guess I've never considered that a tree could talk! Mammals, birds, and reptiles, yes . . . but trees?"

Ruby responded with patience, and I sensed a chuckle. *All of that ability is coming. Be patient. Connecting with me is part of the recalibration process.*

For a split second, I half-questioned my sanity. *Am I really talking to a tree or is this all in my mind? After all, I've been through a lot emotionally in these past few years and haven't been myself lately.*

To test myself, I decided to ask Ruby questions that I could easily verify through other means. I began with the most basic one.

"What kind of tree are you?" I queried.

She answered: *Red pine.*

Hmmmm . . . a red pine named Ruby? Well, that's right on the nose.

Later that evening, I researched the species of tree and, to my surprise, confirmed that Ruby was, in fact, a red pine. The next day when I walked out to the yard, I saw something that I hadn't noticed previously. Ruby was one amongst a grouping of trees whose canopies overlapped. The top of her canopy was missing.

"Ruby, what happened to your top?" I asked.

As if on cue, I heard her answer: *A big wind snapped it off.*

the next time I saw my landlord, he was able to verify this detail.

These question-and-answer sessions between Ruby and me continued for a couple of weeks. Each time, I was astounded by her answers and even more so by the fact that she was always correct. Being able to verify the answers really built my trust in Ruby. This eventually led to my asking her questions around the next steps to take in rebuilding my life.

Gradually, my relationship with Ruby transformed into a genuine friendship. She even began to introduce me to the other trees in my yard, and a whole new world began to open up for me—one that was increasingly filled with magic, possibility, and deep connection.

Not long after my 30-day experiment with Ruby, I had a mystical encounter with an animal who had crossed over into spirit and wanted me to convey a message to its human owner. My tree friend was right again. The guidance that came through Ruby resulted in a series of synchronistic events that began to unfold in the direction of my deepest desire.

Just as she had promised, my dream of speaking with the animal world has come true. Not only do I communicate with animals, I also help others around the world understand the messages coming from the animals and nature.

To this day, the trees continue to be my closest friends, confidants, and teachers. I'm eternally grateful for Ruby's willingness to reach out and share her wisdom with a doubtful human.

Ana Maria Vasquez

HEALING JOY

I reach out for her trunk as though it is my only life raft in the midst of a raging ocean storm. Feeling the stabilizing connection to both tree and earth in my hands, a loving energy surrounds me, bringing quiet and calm to my sobbing. I'm not as alone as I feel. I'm grateful for the gentle, comforting presence of this wise, Divine being, friend, and confidant in tree form, whom I have come to know through the seasons of life that we have shared together.

Three years ago, when I first moved into this home and walked out into the backyard, I saw the five trees planted within the small strip of soil lying along the back fence of my home, as I would see any grouping of trees. Nothing seemed out of the ordinary at first glance.

I started to walk back inside, but something stopped me. Turning around, my attention was drawn to the center tree. I walked over and knelt down to read the tag attached to the trunk: Santa Rosa plum tree. I glanced up at the branches, and back down at the tag.

Hmmm, it's interesting that there aren't any leaves on this tree, I thought. Looking around, the other four trees seemed to be flourishing. I returned

Part Two

inside without giving it further thought, but each time I went out to the backyard, I felt an energetic draw to sit near this plum tree.

My curiosity about her barren branches grew until one day, while taking a few quiet moments to enjoy the warm sunshine, a story dropped in.

"What is your name?" I asked the tree.

You can call me Joy.

This name seemed so paradoxical to the story that I now suddenly knew, one of grief and loss. The couple who had previously lived in the home and had planted Joy and the other trees was gone. The husband had passed and his wife required the additional care of an assisted living facility. Joy was her favorite tree and she took great delight in her.

Joy was now grieving the loss of the family she had known and had watched over in this home. Although it was late summer, there were no leaves on her branches because it was her winter, a barren time in honor of this loss.

Week after week through the fall and winter seasons, I especially felt drawn to sit with Joy while practicing reiki meditations with a loving, healing intention. As spring began to bloom, so, too, did small green buds on her branches. Bright, green leaves eventually blossomed and remained until autumn, when it was time for the leaves to naturally fall.

The following spring brought not only an abundance of leaves, but also a bloom of small, white flowers. These beautiful flowers were like medicine for my heart and soul. The bold yet delicate white petals against the vibrant green leaves had a captivating, sweet-smelling fragrance that brought a lightness and calm to my heart.

Mid-summer, a new gift arrived . . . deep reddish-purple plums. It soon became a plum fest, with a daily ritual and celebration of gathering ripe plums, washing, sorting, and creating in the kitchen with them. Each day, as I collected the plums, I said, *Thank you, Joy, for this beautiful gift of plums. They are so wonderful to have.* I would then continue this conversation by sharing all that I was creating with them, as though I was talking with a friend over tea. I sensed her delight even more, as though it was multiplying with each fruit she produced.

I cherished the gift of witnessing her transformation from barren branches to a plethora of plums. Her sweet, juicy plums were nourishment for my body and the partnership growing between us was nourishment for my heart and soul, which I needed more than I realized.

Years after those first offerings of loving energy were sent to her through reiki, she was returning the offering of being a healing, loving presence as I experienced my own grieving process. It became my new daily ritual to sit next to her with my hand gently resting on her trunk.

Many days, feeling overwhelmed and exhausted from all that I was going through, I would lie underneath her branches, and ask for support from the earth, the sun, and the trees in healing my heart.

At times, I would share my worries, fears, and concerns, and other times I preferred intentional silence, tuning into the internal sound of my breath or externally to the breath of the earth moving through the wind. I felt this grounding, solid energy of the earth beneath me, the steadiness of her trunk next to me, and the warm, healing energy of the sunlight delicately filtering through her branches as they danced in the wind above. Taking all of this in, I could feel my body, mind, and spirit recharging.

This time became my daily way of finding calm in what felt like a storm. Joy was always there to share a word of wisdom if I asked for it. Questions that I brought to our time together were often about how, what, and why. *How do I handle . . . What should I do about . . . What is my next step . . . Why is this happening?*

Often, it was in this space next to her that I received the guidance I was asking for. After just a short time together, I would bring myself to standing once again, feeling more solid in my body, focused, and rejuvenated both physically and emotionally.

One day, during our afternoon connection time, I shared some news with her that I had not been wanting to face.

Joy, at the end of the summer, I will have to leave this home, I explained.

Nothing within me wanted this change, and yet it was happening. I feared the future, where I would go, what I would do, and losing this connection and friendship with Joy. I sat quietly with her, breathing with the sadness that I felt in sharing this news.

It then occurred to me to ask for her help. What if there could be a tree on the land of my next home that I could begin to energetically connect with now, not only for friendship, but also for help in finding my next home? What if it could find *me*? My heart began to beat faster and I could feel my energy rising with hope as I considered this possibility.

"Joy, could you help me connect with a tree that will be on the land of my next home?" I sensed that her assistance was already beginning, and all I had to do was be open to it.

"Joy, I want you and the other trees to know that I'm holding an intention that the people who will come to live in this home after me will care for you just as much and even more than I have. What kind of people would you like to come to this home?"

What came to mind was the idea of a family. I saw an image of small children coming out to the yard to play and delighting in the fruit growing on the trees. I sensed Joy's love for children and desire for a family with small children to live in the home, which she could witness growing up together. I assured her I would hold that intention.

Summer was here again and with it an abundant crop of plums. There seemed to be twice as many plums as the previous year, ripening faster than I could keep up with eating and cooking. It was time to share.

I reached out through local neighborhood networks with news that I had more than 10 pounds of ripe, juicy Santa Rosa plums. For weeks, my kitchen counter was filled with plums as I cleaned, sorted, and organized them, all the while sharing my gratitude with Joy for her delicious gifts.

One Friday afternoon in late July, a woman in a nearby neighborhood came to pick up the last two boxes of plums. As I handed her the boxes, she said, "There's a single woman who lives in the home behind me. She has three small children and they don't have much money. I'll be sharing a box of plums with them, so I'm sure they'll be eaten quickly."

As soon as she said this, I thought, *Joy wanted a family and children to enjoy her fruit. It's already happening!*

After closing the door, I excitedly rushed out to share this news with her. "Joy, she's sharing your plums with children!"

I felt her beaming energy of pure delight. With my hands over my heart, I smiled, looked up to the sky, and gave thanks.

For me, this moment felt like a victory in the midst of a time filled with strife, struggle, and heartache. I thought back to all that I had shared with Joy over the years ... the tears, uncertainty, fear, doubt, celebration, joy, dreams, and desires. But now, our conversations and connection were no longer just about me walking out to my backyard each day and connecting with this Divine being in tree form. It had not only shifted something within me and within her, but had moved beyond the small space of this backyard and out into the world around us. Like circular ripples of water moving outward when a pebble is dropped into it, it was becoming something so much greater than I ever knew it would.

It was a cool and dreary morning, and there was a light mist in the air, but I wasn't going to miss this opportunity to enjoy my last meal in this home while sitting with Joy. Grasping a warm, steamy mug of tea in my hands, I closed my eyes, breathing in deeply the cool, misty air while savoring this moment. It had been a long and busy week, filled with packing, driving loads back and forth, placing items into storage, cleaning, and organizing. I wished for a life that felt normal. My mind had been filled with moving details for as

Part Two

long as I could remember. I wanted this peaceful moment to last forever, but was fighting within myself to enjoy it, when the sadness of losing this safe, peaceful place of connection with Joy was so prevalent.

I hadn't said anything out loud, but she must have tuned into my thoughts, because I heard, *You can meet with me whenever you want.* My attention was quickly brought back to the present. Lost in my wandering thoughts, I wasn't sure I fully heard what she had said. My eyes suddenly glanced over to a leaf resting on the ground near her trunk.

"Is this for me to take?"

Just hold this leaf in your hands and it will be just like we are sitting together. We can meet anytime. That is part of the magic.

"What magic?"

It's the magic of new beginnings. It only looks like an ending, but our connection is timeless so it is always a beginning.

Clasping the leaf in between my hands, I quietly allowed the loving energy of this beautiful gift to soak in.

"How can I feel the magic when I feel so sad?"

Just allow it. Always say yes to the magic.

I thought back to advice she had given me once when I shared with her about a decision I was making. *Stand strong, grow tall, shine your light. Whatever choice you make, you have to allow it to be good. Allow the light to shine on it. Don't crowd it out with doubt and fear. Make space for the light by trusting it. Trusting yourself is what creates a great outcome no matter what you choose.*

"Thank you for reminding me of that."

I took a deep breath and sat silently with Joy for a few more minutes, allowing myself to take in her words more fully. As I did, the heaviness in my heart lifted as I opened to receive the magic of this new beginning.

Jill Landry

THE SURRENDER

*M*y younger brother, Ryan, and I were great friends who shared a passion for the outdoors. We would often hike together and explore lovely landscapes off the beaten path. Nature has taught us so much—when to hold on, how to be patient, and when to let go. I needed nature's wisdom more desperately than ever after Ryan's life was abruptly taken in a car accident.

A few months after his transition, I take to the woods on one of our favorite trails in search of some way to ease my aching heart. The beautiful, blue sky perks up my spirits and beckons me onto this well-trodden pathway alongside a stream. Instantly, I feel a familiar wonder as I meander amongst the swaying hemlocks. My heart swells from the beauty of the sunlight squeezing in between the branches. Everything feels familiar and nurturing.

Close to a mile into my trek, I sense an urge to stop and go down to the flowing water where a giant rock comes into view. It seems like the perfect place to stretch out and absorb the beauty surrounding me. Heeding the call, I hop on a few rocks and lie down, breathing deeply and enjoying the warmth of the sun on my body. To my chagrin, I'm not able to completely relax, as my mind is preoccupied with the slight downward slant of the surface beneath me. I don't feel comfortable or safe.

Nevertheless, I'm determined to stay. I ask myself what I need to feel at ease, and soon realize that I can sink my body and energy into the rock for stability. So, I sink into the rock . . . and the more I become anchored, the more I relax . . . and the more I relax, the more I sink . . . until I can feel myself *as* the rock. I am fully myself and fully the rock, completely grounded. The base of my being enmeshes with the mud and earth under the stream. I can feel the cool water brushing around my sides to join the whole of itself once again. A feeling of elation washes over me.

Soon, I find that I am not limited to joining with just the rock underneath me. As I shift myself over to the smaller rock across the water, I experience its own weight, girth, and stability. I can feel a difference in the personality or consciousness of this rock. My mind focuses on the feel of the water skirting around me, and I somehow shift and *become* the water.

I am the essence of joyful, jubilant waterdrops flying through the air, each one rejoining the stream below into a whole new, deeper experience of gladness at that merging. With an absolute sense of joy in my heart, I am me and I am the water. Integrated. Individuated. Yet melded within consciousness. As soon as I begin to think about how amazing this experience is, I come back into my physical body, feeling complete.

I jump off the rock and back onto the trail . . . but, oh . . . what a different *me* is on this trail! Everything in my awareness is heightened, shimmering, and loving. I am able to instantly feel the Divine in all that I see. I savor the essence of everything that my eyes fall upon. And I feel seen, as well, in the same way that I am seeing everything else. I delight in this precious gift of finally knowing myself, fully embodied.

I walk on in this state of awareness for approximately two miles until I come to a bridge leading to the return trail on the other side of the water. Still in a blissful state, I cross the bridge and spot a marker for a trail that Ryan and I were going to hike the next time he came home.

The grief hits me so deeply, so unexpectedly. We will never get to explore this trail. We will never hike together ever again. I resist the sadness welling up in me, which feels doubly intense after having just been feeling so incredible. I want to stay in this beautiful, blissful space instead of acknowledge my grief.

Attempting to shrug it off, I set off on the trail, determined to find my way back to the heaven that I had been experiencing moments earlier. After taking only a few steps, I notice a beautiful, lone wildflower. I have a great urge to pick it and carry it with me on the hike, but I hesitate, knowing that it will die more quickly if I pluck it from its life source. With a heaviness I can't explain, I bend down and pick the flower then instantly regret my action.

What should I do now? I ponder. *And why am I so emotional about this flower?* Somewhere in my mind I know that my panic is connected to my grief. I gather some leaves, soak them in the stream, and wrap them around the stem to extend its life a bit longer.

This does nothing to quell my sadness. As I walk, bewildered, tears pour out of me. I cling to the flower, willing it to stay alive. Yet each time I glance at it, I know it's going to die, which brings on more sobbing from the core of my being.

Glancing at the water, I intuitively know that I need to let go of the flower on my own accord by placing it in the creek and allowing it to flow downstream. When I reach the end of the trail, I locate the perfect spot to place the flower in the stream.

Feeling a subtle wisp of tranquility, I realize that the stream can keep the flower alive much better than I ever could. Willing myself to be ready, I gently place the flower in the creek and say goodbye . . . but I hadn't quite meant it . . . and to my surprise, the flower gets caught on something along the way and stays within my sight.

In this quiet, precious moment, held in the loving embrace of Nature, I hear my brother speak.

Take your time, Ryan says. *I will be here for as long as you need.*

With that, I am able to smile, tell Ryan I love him, and truly let him go . . . and with that, the flower floats on down the stream.

A.K. Baker

ERICA'S TREE

BOOM ... boom ... boom ... boom . . . BOOM ... boom ... boom ... boom . . .

The four-beat rhythm of my deerskin drum thundered through the crisp winter air. As I sat on the cold stones of the landscaped wall, the drumming slowed down my mind and breath to mesh with the sentience of the tall Canadian cherry tree. My intention was to journey to the spirit of this tree in the lower world, where it was residing in the safety of the earth, protected from our cold Midwest winter.

Before beginning my journey, I asked permission from the tree's spirit to come visit and felt that the answer was yes. I wanted to formally introduce myself and thank him for his gifts to our family and to ask a special personal favor.

This Canadian cherry tree was planted in a large circle of earth when it was just a thin sapling. The mound of dirt was then surrounded by a short wall of gray paver stones. The tree has since grown to a towering 30 feet and is the striking focal point of our expansive front yard. Its glowing copper bark sheds paper-like curls from its massive branches, which arch downward as they cover a 40-foot diameter, shading the stone wall and grass beyond.

Part Two

Thousands of oval, emerald-green leaves glow in the blazing sun like a Tiffany lamp. The broad shadow cast by the canopy is so dense that walking beneath it is like entering into a curtained room. In the spring, this tree is adorned by a cream-colored blanket of blossoms, which morph into tiny dark cherries in the summer months.

Our beloved Canadian cherry is a sentinel tree, the first tree at the entrance to our property. He guards our land and alerts his fellow trees to the presence of visitors and danger. To me, the most important contribution of this stunning tree is that it was a witness to my granddaughter's short life.

We now call this tree Erica's Tree, named after our little granddaughter who grew up under its branches. As a baby, her grandpa would bring her outside on warm Saturday mornings, their special time together, and lay her on a small quilt placed on the dewy grass under the tree's shade canopy. The outstretched branches hung low enough to be touched when he lifted her tiny body up to feel the smooth, cool surface of a soft leaf. Grandpa would entertain Erica with bright shiny toys that rolled or rocked and played happy sounds, as he talked to her with silly voices to coax her to smile and coo.

As Erica grew, she would determinedly crawl off the blanket towards the wall and pull herself up to bounce on her short legs, her almond-shaped, brown eyes sparkling with glee. Later, she took tentative sideways steps as her chubby baby hands gripped the top of the stones for balance. When her toddler legs became sturdier and her personality bolder, Erica climbed upon the wall and walked around the tree, holding my hand, laughing, and squealing with delight. As she neared her second birthday, Erica enjoyed picking up tiny twigs that had fallen off the tree and throwing them back to the trunk at the center of the stone ring. She so enjoyed this game that, of course, we doting grandparents retrieved the twigs for her to throw again and again.

In January, shortly after her second birthday, Erica contracted a mysterious illness. By early February, she had begun a grueling stay at a children's hospital that lasted into April. The team of doctors were baffled as they tested her for all the usual childhood illnesses and the results yielded no definitive answers. We were devastated to helplessly watch our smart, active, happy two-year-old's brain fade away by unchecked inflammation. Each week, she declined physically and mentally until she was labeled comatose, and we brought her home into hospice care.

Yet even in her new silent state, Erica shared a connection with her tree, her lifelong playmate. When the snow melted and the late spring temperatures allowed, I placed her still and limp body into a soft-backed stroller and wheeled her into the shade of her tree. As I sat on the top of the stone wall, I told her about the weather of the day and the events in the neighborhood. I'd share nursery rhymes, read her favorite story books aloud, and sing songs in my faltering, off-key voice until it broke from sadness, and I could sing no more.

Because Erica was unable to move her body, I picked up tiny twigs and fallen leaves to place in her curled hands. When I did so, she slightly opened her eyes and seemed to acknowledge these familiar items. As the weeks passed and the illness progressed, her eyes no longer opened. Yet knowing this was a favorite place of hers to be, we visited the tree often.

As her conscious mind shut down, I felt certain that her soul continued to flit in and out of her body, and she knew when she was in the cool shade of her tree. Our precious Erica left us in late July, shortly before her third birthday.

BOOM ... boom ... boom... boom . . . BOOM ... boom ... boom ... boom.

The tones vibrated from my drum as I shifted into the slightly altered state that would allow my subconscious mind to begin the journey. It was the winter after Erica passed as I entered the lower world to find the spirit of the cherry tree. Once I had connected in, I thanked him for his gifts to our family beyond shade and life-sustaining oxygen: comfort, protection, happiness, joy, and growth experiences for Erica.

The tree told me that he is known as Strong Heart, but knew that I call him Erica's Tree, and gave his approval. He appreciated that I recognized his responsibilities and importance as a sentinel tree. He understood his significance to our family and acknowledged his close relationship with Erica. He shared his own happiness at spending time with Erica and that he absorbed her sweet child energy, shared in our joy with her antics, and enjoyed being the cause of so much entertainment.

Strong Heart conveyed to me that Erica visits our family often and stops by to say hello and dance upon the wall beneath his branches. That is when I asked him for my favor: Would he allow us to relandscape the space within his stone wall into a memorial garden for Erica?

I waited a few moments, then distinctly felt a strong *yes*. Both relieved and elated, I again thanked Strong Heart, quickened the drum beat rhythm and began the return journey to my own world.

A few months later, in spring, we started the task of relandscaping. A few original shrubs had expired during the especially cold winter with little snow cover to insulate their roots from the deep frost. Grandpa carefully pulled out the dead shrubs and their roots without disturbing the cherry tree's own root system.

We prepared the soil to plant several patches of bright green phlox, perennials that would grace us each spring with pink and purple blossoms, Erica's favorite colors. I placed each plant's root ball into the rich earth, watering it with my tears. My overwhelming emotions served as fertilizer, feeding the plants with sorrow, joy, and gratitude.

She wasn't here on this earth for long, but Erica had an impact on many, including her tree friend. Erica's Tree lives here still and is an ongoing legacy to her short life. A small pink Adirondack chair gifted to us by a special friend sits as the focal point in her memorial garden. The chair is flanked by ceramic animals representing those she loved most: squirrels, rabbits, frogs, and turtles. Behind the pink chair are solar lights in flower shapes, and a crescent moon with stars. As I look out the front windows of my home in the evenings, the glowing lights in the memorial garden comfort me. I feel that when Erica comes, she sits in her pink chair and visits with her tree and animals.

I often sit under Erica's Tree, on the little wall next to her chair and listen to Strong Heart share his adventures with her, his leaves softly rustling in the gentle breeze.

Cheri Evjen

THE WHIRL OF A LEAF

*A*utumn was always my favorite season of the year, even as far back to when I was five years old—the leaves turning orange and yellow and red, the unexpected breezes whipping up from nowhere, and filling my decorated cigar box with my favorite pencils in anticipation of the school year.

Growing up my family home was close enough to our school, St. Savior's, that my sister and I could walk to it each day, sometimes with other kids in the neighborhood. This particular day, I walked alone.

The final bell rang and the doors swung open to release me from my first-grade class. Unintentionally, I was not joined by any of my friends who walked home in the same direction. I hadn't even noticed, as my attention was caught up in the autumn air and fragrance of the changing trees.

As I walked, it felt like nature was dancing and singing. Like being enthralled in a great theater performance, my senses were captivated by the beauty of the sound and movement.

By the time I was about halfway home, I felt an inner urge to be part of the dance; in fact, it was so strong that I couldn't imagine *not* being a part of it. So, I started to whirl, losing all sense of myself in the larger nature choreography that was happening around me.

The rest of the way home, I spun and spun in sheer delight. When I reached my driveway at the end of the cul-de-sac, the whirling stopped . . . but the bliss did not.

Coming slowly back to my senses, I observed how incredibly happy I felt in every part of myself. As I rested in that, I took in the world around me. Passively yet actively, I inhaled and exhaled the street, the grass, the dandelions, the trees, the parked cars, and the sky.

A particular tree caught my attention across the road in my neighbor's yard. It seemed to gleefully shout, *Look at me!*

The next few moments were ineffable, as my gaze was taken into the tree . . . and all else faded around it. One leaf pulled me in tightly, wrapping itself around my soul as it teetered, still hanging onto its home and quivering towards breaking away. The leaf and I merged and my soul moved as it moved.

Then it broke off its small branch and began its circling descent to the ground.

Unexpectedly, while in this state of deep, abiding bliss, an anguish arose within me as the leaf and I floated to the ground. A question arose unsolicited and with such sadness that I could not put into words.

Is that all there is? We are just here to die? We are born, and all of life is moving towards dying?

As these questions burst forth, my Beloved—my name for what I would later come to understand as Consciousness—caused all time to stop. I did not sense a Presence that was separate from me . . . only a deep caring that did not want me to have one moment of such anguish.

As time stopped, the veil lifted and a part of me opened completely into a revelation: *The leaf is in God and God is in the leaf* . . . though even the concept of *in* didn't quite describe it. This revelation dissolved the question and the sadness, and opened me to an all-consuming insight: My life and all of life is about one thing . . . being and becoming in God.

Incredible joy interpenetrated my being, and the clarity of this mystical dance with Nature has remained as the context for all of my surrender into a timeless grace. Even to this day, it continues to reveal the Eternal each moment . . . through nights of confusion and change, and days of ease and insight.

Rev. Kimberly Braun

THE FEAR ROCKS

On the road to Flagstaff with my husband, I was struck with a severe anxiety attack. We had been traveling fulltime in our RV, and while I enjoyed discovering new places, it left me feeling somewhat unbalanced. Simultaneously, I had been going through a phase where my energetic sensitivity had shifted; as a result, I felt overwhelmed without fully realizing why.

Overcome with extreme paranoia and fear of everyone and everything, I decided to take a few days to do a solitary healing retreat in Sedona, a place that has always calmed and inspired me.

Catching sight of Sedona's resplendent red rocks, high mesas, and rocky cliffs is always incredibly stunning, and this time was no exception.

"Please help me!" I cried out to the mountains, throwing myself on their healing mercy.

By the time I settled into my hotel room then headed over to the Sedona Creative Life Center, I had regained enough of my composure to get out of the vehicle and walk around. Still inwardly praying for Divine guidance, something immediately caught my attention through the trees: the top of a gazebo located near the rear parking lot. Curious to see what was back there

Part Two

and following my intuition, I meandered towards it and saw a beautifully landscaped space filled with stately trees and flowers of many colors. A sign at the entrance said Peace Garden.

Ah . . . just what I need, I thought. Entering the manicured grounds, a palpable sense of grace filled my being and beckoned me to walk off the stone path towards a canopy of tree branches. The wind whispered through the shimmering leaves of the canopy, seeming to dance and speak in the voice of nature itself.

Under this canopy, a 12-foot circle of nine impressive rocks appeared before me, ranging in height from about two to four feet. Intuitively, the words Fear Rocks came to me. As I reverently entered the circle, the air felt alive and time seemed to stop. Instantly, I understood that the purpose of these stones was to help heal and transform fear by listening and holding space for my innermost feelings that were manifesting as extreme anxiety.

One by one, as I stood in front of and focused on each rock, I received information through my claircognizance about the specific types of fear that each of the nine stones helps to steward: rejection, after death, nightmares, aggression, sickness, violent death, hatred, hopelessness, and helplessness. Luckily, I'd brought a notebook with me, so I scrambled to jot down all of the details that were streaming through my intuition from the Fear Rocks.

The trees chimed in and reminded me that these nine fears are shared human experiences, and that we all encounter them in some way, shape, or form. Walking into the center of the stone circle, I felt an immediate sense of relief in the profound surrender of allowing the rocks to hold my burdens. My prayer to the red rocks had been witnessed and answered.

It was humbling to understand that the rocks' solid and majestic energy had the ability to ground, diffuse, heal, and transform my human fears. They imparted to me that I could talk, meditate, and pray with them at any time after leaving the garden and from a distance.

Offering the trees and the Fear Rocks my sincere thanks, I exited the Peace Garden in ... well, peace. Transformed by this experience of the Divine in nature and my heart bursting open to receive, my inward healing weekend could now begin.

Tracy Sheppard

TREES, HORSES, AND TRANSFORMATION

I had no idea that trees were so powerful until one day, while sitting near one, I felt an incredible rush of bliss. This made me curious to learn more about how trees are interconnected, grow together, speak to each other, and provide much more than shelter and shade.

That mystical bliss experience was still on my mind one day while working as an equine-partnered coach at a horse ranch. I was overjoyed to discover a special tree growing right inside of the turnout where I was hosting my client sessions. At first glance, this tree looked simple and ordinary, but I knew there was also something special about it.

A grandmother had come to the ranch with her grandchildren to work with me and the horses. Her grandson was pretty jazzed to meet my thoroughbred mare, Lindsey, but the granddaughter was timid and fearful. She mostly hid behind her grandma and stared at the ground. I had never seen that much of a fear response from a child around Lindsey, who was always very gentle and loved kids.

Not wanting this little girl to feel pushed to face her fear, often the way I was as a child, I listened to what Lindsey might have to communicate. She suggested that I take a walk with the child over to the donkey paddock. I wasn't sure why but when we got there, I noticed another special tree, just as strong and beautiful as the one in the turnout. Intuitively, I knew what to do.

"Would you be willing to hug the tree?" I asked the girl. "It wants to help you with your fear of the horse."

Shyly, she nodded yes.

I encouraged her to put her arms around the trunk, and visualize her fear dissolving into its roots and being composted by the soil. She played along with this, holding onto the tree with all of her tiny might while keeping her eyes tightly closed. After a few minutes, as she stepped back from the trunk with a little grin on her face, she appeared to have a new glow of confidence.

Upon doing this simple process, the girl was able to greet the donkeys up close—which, of course, are smaller than horses, so it served to warm her up a bit more for being around my mare.

"How are you feeling now?" I asked, as I held her delicate hand and led her back to the turnout.

"I don't feel scared anymore," she offered ... the first time she had spoken since arriving at the ranch.

With that confirmation, I walked her right up to Lindsey, who was patiently waiting to give her some equine love.

Reaching out to touch Lindsey's mane, with her grandmother happily looking on, the girl broke out in a giggle and began to cuddle Lindsey from the side.

"Would you like to groom her?" I asked.

"Can I?"

"You can!"

For the next half hour or so, the family spent time with Lindsey, as I watched in awe at how quickly the tree had transmuted the girl's energy from fear to confidence. Even Lindsey looked at me with a glance that seemed to say, *Good work!* I snapped some photographs of this lovely family and the session ended with the girl hugging the other magical tree in the turnout we were in with Lindsey.

"You can always ask the trees for help if you feel afraid, and they will change your fear into love," I said to her in parting. Everyone left with huge smiles and I felt complete wonder at what had just transpired.

After this incredible transformation, I wanted to experience this healing energy from the trees for myself and soon had the perfect opportunity to do so at the ranch. Feeling very nervous about a demonstration that I had to give to the CEO of a big conference, I brought my mare, Lindsey, and some other horses into the turnout, went over to hug the special tree, and shared with her my nervousness about the presentation.

Please help me to feel calm and confident, I spoke to the tree through my inner voice. *I want to do my best. This is an important potential deal for my business.*

Standing there for a short while as the horses watched, my breathing spontaneously slowed and a massive surge of love began to flow through my body as it had the day of my bliss experience. For several minutes, I basked in the essence of profound joy, eventually stepping away from the tree in a calm yet highly confident state.

When the time came to deliver the demo to the CEO and his team, I was able to remain centered and self-assured, even when Lindsey stepped on my client's foot—the first time that had ever happened! Instead of losing my cool and freaking out, I gently moved Lindsey's leg and intuitively knew to ask the client what was coming up for him.

As he sat down, I could tell that a flood of new ideas was coming into his consciousness. He paused to reflect, then started to speak about love. It's almost as if the love that the magical tree fed into me was being transferred to the client, with an assist from Lindsey, too. The whole team left that day feeling connected and amazed at the power of the horses and nature.

Within a couple of weeks, I learned that I had secured a deal to work with this team annually, and I have since assisted numerous CEOs and CMOs of top brands as a result of this connection. My favorite part of the Divine unfoldment of this client's work was when I started to see the language around the marketing of their conference rapidly shift to focus on messages around love, higher potential, and new possibilities. I personally believe that the trees' energy—and the horses—helped to create these outcomes, as these messages about the sacredness of all life were delivered through my work with them.

Since these profound experiences, I have never looked at trees in the same way. When I feel that clients are open to working with a tree as a healer and transmuter of energy, I offer it to them in their sessions.

I've since moved away from that geographic area but later discovered that the land used to be home to Native Americans. That made sense to me because I often felt that they were watching over my sessions and giving their approval that my clients and I were seeing the deeper truths of nature.

Today, I am blessed to be working on a ranch in Colorado that also has sacred trees. One day, while sitting under a patch of trees, I heard one of them begin to share that they are a chakra system of exactly seven trees in a curved row, similar to how the spine curves upward. Often, I've noticed that the horses will stand next to the crown chakra with their heads and third eyes pointed at the trunk.

Other days, I'll awaken with a surge of love pulsing through me, and when I get to the ranch, they are standing around the heart chakra in a line spanning outward into the field, all connected and receiving. It's a beautiful sight to behold.

I've also seen my mare, Phoenix, sitting on the ground, especially in the snow, by the solar plexus chakra, receiving stomach support. This is the same spot where I was able to mount her while she was seated, and we trusted each other enough that she could stand and walk around with me on her back without any tack—which was one of my life goals to experience with a horse. This particular tree clearly shows up when willpower and trust is needed.

I'm grateful that I have seen the true nature of Nature, and the healing properties and power of trees. I talk to trees frequently now and often look to include all of nature—especially the elements, wind, sun, mountains, land, winged critters, and, of course, trees—in my client sessions, so many more people can see what I see and experience the invisible world. It helps everyone fall more deeply in love with nature, which makes my heart full.

Kate Neligan

A WILD AND RAGING STORM

The sun peaked over the horizon as my friends and I piled into the car for a fun, out-of-town drive. We were going on a walk together at a nature preserve, and were excited to learn about native plants and various ecosystems.

The sky was slightly overcast as we met our nature guide and started down a weathered, wooden walkway into the dense woods. With so many interesting trees and wildflowers along the way, my focus was drawn into the up-close details of the flora and fauna. After wandering through a swampy area and coming onto a path that bordered a large pasture, I had gotten so enthralled with studying everything around me that I realized I had fallen behind the group.

"Hey Anne, keep up with us!" my friends called to me. "You're missing what our guide is sharing with us!"

By the next half hour, we had rambled quite a distance from the main building. The further we walked, the darker and heavier the cloudy sky became. As a transplanted Midwesterner who grew up with some crazy storms, I started to get a little concerned . . . but the trees and plants along the route continued to draw me in, as if I was directly connecting with their energy.

By the time we had passed clump after clump of palmetto bushes at the edge of a forested area, I was no longer listening to the guide's narration. The darkening sky now had most of my attention.

Suddenly, one of the palmettos on my left rustled ... and not due to wind. I distinctly heard a message coming from it through my inner knowing: A violent storm was indeed about to hit, and we would be in danger if we didn't take cover.

Turn around now! the palmetto impressed on me. It was a command, not a suggestion.

Did this palmetto bush just give me a warning? It took a moment to get my head around that. The message came with such force that I stood there, shocked, not knowing how to explain to our leader that we needed to turn back in the direction of the building.

I didn't need to, as in the very next breath, our guide got the message, too.

In a booming voice, almost like thunder itself, she yelled out the same words that the palmetto had spoken to me.

"We need to turn around! Now!"

Everyone in the group pivoted and began to high-tail it back towards the main building.

As soon as we changed direction, curiously, the incoming storm seemed to blow over and the skies lightened. Intuitively, I sensed that we had altered the progression of the storm by changing our actions. Some kind of mystical interaction was occurring between us and nature.

With this temporary reprieve from the storm, we continued onward towards a nearby shelter and when we were about 100 feet from the tiny building, the sky suddenly turned black and heavy again. A deluge of rain began to pummel the ground, causing everyone to break into a sprint. We

Divine Experiences with Trees, Plants, Stones and Landscapes

barely made it through the doorway of the shelter when thunder cracked nearby and lightning ripped open the sky.

All of us huddled in this tiny space, packed tight but safe. Being the last person in the shelter, there was little room for me so I scootched in the door frame under the wide eaves. The rain pelting the tin roof sounded like machine guns rattling. Tall pine trees bent and swayed in the powerful winds. Leaves and other debris went flying and swirling into the air. The palmettos and other bushes thrashed about wildly. Lightning repeatedly struck close to our little haven, and the thunder was continuous and deafening. It was as if the woods themselves were raging.

Yet there was great beauty in the storm, and its magic lured me out onto the porch swing under the eaves. Watching the wind blowing, the rain pouring, the vegetation glistening, the lightning flashing, I felt peaceful, present, and at one with everything around me, both observer and participant. The raindrops shattering onto objects eased me into a deeply relaxed state. The sound and motion of the swing beneath me was equally hypnotic. For some time, I stayed in this space of oneness with the storm, watching puddles form under the nearby oaks.

Eventually, my friends decided to make a mad dash for the car and head home. Saddened to leave the storm, I felt yanked out of this special experience, and as we drove back to town, I tried to fathom what had just happened.

A palmetto bush had warned me, and everyone else, of danger. I wondered if the guide consciously knew where the urge to turn back came from, or if she had simply acted on the warning. Either way, Nature came to the rescue as the storm temporarily let up to give us deliberate safe passage to shelter.

Filled with gratitude and wonder, this unforgettable nature walk opened me to new ways of seeing life. The possibilities suddenly seemed endless.

Anne Cederberg

TREE SPIRITS AMONG US

I stack four pieces of wood across my arm and walk deliberately towards the fire. Anticipation builds as I watch the sun slide behind the tree line. Along with 28 other men, we quicken our preparations for the evening's sweat lodge, the centerpiece here on night three of my first vision quest. We move unrehearsed, observing conversational silence, feeling our way.

My senses are peaked in this setting. I smell the ripe tree bark that gives structure to the lodge and hear moisture hiss and pop away from the heating wood and stone. My eyes widen as I approach the woodpile. A random swing of an axe has split one log, leaving it with an unmistakable figure in the grain. I smile, delighted to see an eagle's tufted head with a protruding beak.

Courage, I say to myself. *Yes, I could use a dose or two of eagle medicine to complete this quest.*

In a gasp of childlike joy, I take the eagle's head from the woodpile and set it aside. I try to show a friend, but she sees it differently. I awaken to a simple truth: We each see with what artists call the "beholder's share." No two images leave the same impression. In that moment, I find acceptance, and the idea that my view of the world and what I see is mine to explore.

Part Two

Sight is not something I take for granted. A cataract left me blind in my right eye from birth. That eye remains extremely sensitive to light. I am constantly reminded of the deficit. Needless to say, what I see and don't see is important. What is spoken and not spoken matters, as well.

Growing up in a family of nine, I experienced sexual abuse as a child. Few in my family saw or spoke of it, or care now to look into the immense, shadowy energies stirred by the trauma. Yet, somehow, I've held tight to my desire to fully feel, respond, reflect, and potentially heal. This vision quest was all about preparing a sacred place where I could ask for what I needed—forgiveness, hope, and even a new vision where I could recapture my innate sense of joy and wonder.

My healing journey with help from nature continued several years later on a trip to San Francisco to visit California's Redwoods. I arrived there to take the next big leap in my journey of recovering my vital energy.

A few steps beyond the gravel parking lot, my senses sharpen as they had on my earlier vision quest. I stand surrounded by sacred space. Nature slows my heartbeat. The sensation of standing at six-feet, eight-inches in height, alongside 250 to 300 feet tall trees gives me comfort. I yield to Tree energy. These old ones have my back.

In one strand, a shaft of light cuts through a small break in the tree canopy and lights up a half-rotted tree. Shadow, line, form, vision. A wizard-like gnome, complete with long hat and white beard, emerges from the wood grain. I pause. That familiar question returns: *Am I seeing what I think I am seeing*? All sense of time stops. I can hear my deep breathing and feel my ease… a whole body feeling of peace.

And then comes a startling sound: a hummingbird hovering six inches from my ears. I stay calm. The hummingbird is no threat. We find a happy co-existence. The remainder of the day brings a similar balance as I ponder the Arab expression, "See if you can find eternity in the hour that passes."

Over the years since that trip to the Redwoods, my curiosity about tree spirits has deepened, but like the growth of a tree, I am taking my time. After several additional vision quests, I realized that my two worlds—seen and unseen—could no longer be ignored. I began to honor what I physically see with my good eye, and what I metaphysically see with my other.

On one particular quest, I lie alone in the woods—solo night—an experience designed to slow one's internal rhythms to match nature's pace and open you to other worlds. As I position myself against a stump, I can feel the deep fissures and crevices in the bark against my shoulders. I smell the dirt around me and the sweet blossoming flowers. The papery leaves rustle in the wind. An occasional chipmunk scurries about foraging for food. As the sun begins to set and shadows start to dance, I see firework displays of light in the woods. Winds change and as the leaves move, faces appear, and disappear, then reappear. I am the guest at a party where everyone wants to greet me. Wow! I experience my first wonder bender! I am getting closer.

I awake in the morning to a warm, earthy smell induced by an overnight rain. As I roll out of my lean-to, heading to breakfast, I am stunned. On the tree directly in front of my sleeping arrangements is a perfectly profiled silhouette of a man . . . the eye, the nose, the neck . . . all masterfully painted by the rain.

I stand euphoric, in total awe. Tears rush down my cheeks, as I become awash with a calming lightness. After some time in the presence of the image and in this curious secret world, I reach for my camera to capture what I know language would fail to describe. Unbeknownst to me, it is the first of hundreds of photos to come in which I document and share how these discernible forest friends reveal themselves to me everywhere. Thousands of otherwise unseen tree spirits, shadow spirits, and water spirits have opened themselves to me, and, in turn, to a life that grows ever fuller with wonder every day.

Part Two

As an abused child, my carefree spirit shouldered a heavy load. Survival required me to hide it for a long time. With equal parts faith and reason, magic and mystery, I've declared that it's safe for that part of my spirit to come out and play, and nature is my truest playmate. I am alive in the trees . . . and they have affirmed . . . that while I was born blind in my right eye, I can see magic in my left.

Dan Cavanaugh

LIVING WITH A WATER SPIRIT

*F*eeling a deep connection with water, I am happy to have a natural stream as a neighbor, the comforting sound of a flowing waterfall nearby, and the deep croaks of frogs all around.

As I meander around the babbling water for the first time since moving to this property, I suddenly sense an upset water being at a bend in the stream. It feels as though there is a giant shield around the area, and a wariness of humans coming into it.

Private property! The water spirit reprimands me through my claircognizance. *Please respect and stand away from this area.*

I sense layers of unconscious abuse of the land from humans over many eons. Some of this pollution is evident, and the sight of it brings uncomfortable feelings of joy mixed with grief. The water needs help, and an impulse to co-create with this ally rises up. I long to see if the stream and I can connect in an invisible field beyond time.

My way of establishing this connection is simple. I bring flowers to a place in the stream, far enough from the guarded realm of the nature spirit to acknowledge my respect for her. Slowly dropping them into the stream one by one, I ask forgiveness then wait . . . soon feeling the persistent resonance of tiny waves rippling out and around the flowers.

Offering blessings, I humbly ask that healing occur and that the circles of resonance around the flowers reach out and touch all of life. Adding sound to my ritual with bells, singing, and chanting, I continue to honor the water spirit, yet do not feel any immediate clearing or shift.

With each small flower that lands and floats in the water, frogs jump towards them from the perimeter of the stream. Small fish swim in close in anticipation of a rare treat. Some of the blooms twirl and dance as I intend that my sincere gesture generates clarity and a clearing.

For the next couple of months, I return to the stream to repeat this flower offering. In amazement, I notice an invitation to enter the water spirit's realm in a particular section. The energy of it feels a bit like stepping across a threshold into an old-fashioned, small parlor where I can sit, observe, and give my full attention to the stream. I am elated. What an honor . . .and yet I hesitate to sit down.

In this moment of trepidation, an owl swoops out of a nearby tree.

This is rare and a breakthrough collaboration, I hear. *Your wish is granted. Go now before it closes.*

While only a tiny part of the realm is open, it's an important beginning. The overture is tentative and delicate. I feel a plea to talk ever so quietly, mostly feeling and listening. My small offering of flowers spins in a small whirlpool, almost too slow and gentle to see the flow. My admiration goes out to the persistent, generous aspect of water, always finding ways to move, however slow and imperceptible.

Days go by with my return visits and prayers until one afternoon, while gazing into the stream, a gentle haze arises from the water. A face approaches me then becomes a being from the water, an ancient one. In awe at this sight, feelings of gratitude and love pour out of me for this being, not only as a partner but as a family and community.

Months more pass and a growing kinship develops with other friends who have come to honor the water. One morning, my messenger owl flies out from an area of the stream with an urgent message: *Please help!*

Uncomfortable feelings well up, as they had that first time I encountered the stream. I soon discover why. As I stroll over to the neighbor's property on the other side of the stream, I notice that he had poisoned a line of trees that were blocking his view of the stream. Their sickened branches had bent low into the stream, transferring this poison into the water.

Seeing once more into the invisible realm of nature, it was obvious that part of my neighbor's realm had shut down again. Feeling sick and upset, I spoke with the water spirit, and it responded with its wisdom.

I will be sick for a while, but the offerings you make and the people you now bring by that sing, place crystals, and bless the water strengthens the field of possibility of healing with humans. Please know that I see that you are here for me, as are others. I have been here a long time, so have patience and stay true to yourself and your commitment.

With that message, I knew that my work with water spirit was not ending—it had only just begun.

Ann Marie Holmes

TIM THE TREE

The summer sun is spectacular, emanating the kind of light that makes me want to rip off my clothes to let my skin drink in its glowing warmth. A sweet gentle breeze, just strong enough to muss my hair, takes the edge off the heat. Magpies chatter, defending their territories, as I stroll aimlessly through Treasury Gardens in Melbourne. The grass is so soft and inviting that I jettison my shoes and venture off the paved pathway. The cool lawn tickles the soles of my feet and I immediately connect to nature.

Oi! My communing is abruptly interrupted. I pivot to see who is there, and I see no one. But clear as day, I'd heard a man's voice trying to get my attention. Am I being reprimanded for walking on the grass?

Oi! The traditional Aussie greeting rings out again, as if someone is looking for loose change or a spare smoke. This time, the inflection is friendly, not off-putting.

Oi! he calls out again.

Okay, what's going on? I wonder. *Is someone hiding behind a tree and taunting me?* I peer in the direction of the call. No one. I scrutinize the park to my right and see fig trees, a fountain, and grassy lawns, but no people. *What the?*

Suddenly, my breathing becomes shallow, my muscles tighten, and I feel a growing uneasiness mixed with confusion. *What does this voice want?*

The call comes again, louder this time. *Oi! You!*

I whirl around once more in search of a person. The voice seems to emanate from directly in front of me, and the only thing in sight is an elm tree. I stare at the tree, which is quite a specular specimen. Calming myself, I take a breath and connect with the earth under my feet.

Wham! Reaching into my very soul, a tractor beam of sensation pulls my focus to this tree. Goosebumps rise on my arms. The elm tree is staring into me. We lock eyes. *Can you lock eyes with a tree?* Excitement mixes with desire. It is the familiar sensation of meeting a soul mate. Currents of unconditional love and deep knowing surge between us. This tree and me.

While experiencing this soul connection, the scene changes. This commonplace elm tree in the park now appears as a carnival of tiny, sparkling lights dancing through its branches and leaves. It's not a trick of the sun or an infestation of fireflies. The tree is literally emitting light and glowing as if lit from the inside.

"Was that you?" I ask the tree out loud.

The answer comes as a distinct voice, yet inside my head. *Yes, you can see me, I can see you.*

After having been a site-whispering shaman for more than 30 years, I've seen a few magical things and communicate with all sorts of entities and ancestors. I've developed an intricate and delicate process of opening my senses to spiritual communication. This conversation, however, is not like a regular spirit chat. I didn't initiate this connection . . . the tree did, and there wasn't any special, sensitive tuning in required on my part. It feels ordinary, like standing barefoot in the park having a normal, albeit telepathic, conversation with an elm tree.

Corny as it sounds, the tree says, *I've seen you here before.* I laugh at the notion of a tree using this pickup line. *Call me Tim.*

What? Tim? That feels way too human, but he interjects, *I've always liked that name.*

Carrying on this somewhat flirtatious banter, I ask, "Do you talk to a lot of humans?"

I do but no one has answered back in a long time. I always try though. One person did reply some time ago, but they haven't come back.

Our conversation continues as Tim invites me to come closer and make physical contact so we can get to know one another better. I come close and give him a hug. Immediately, I dissolve into the body of Tim. My senses shift. I become tall. I feel connected to the whole park. This sensitivity to all the living beings of the park extends in all directions. I simultaneously feel the dry warmth of the sun and cool moisture of the earth. *This is what it feels like to be a tree,* I realize, imagining that the tree is, in turn, feeling what it's like to be me.

In the years since that initial meeting, Tim has maintained a teacher-student relationship with me. He teaches me about living as a tree across all the seasons of the year. In the spring, I learn that Tim is co-sexual. For Tim's species of elm, sex exists beyond the binary of female and male. His flowers are protogynous, meaning that they are able to change their sex at a certain point in the year. In our chat about his gender fluidity, he says, *It's too difficult to explain. Go look it up.*

Using the wood-wide-web, Tim calls me to the park when the timing is right to teach me something about tree life, explaining how he found me in my apartment two kilometers away through the mycelium network. He taught me to photosynthesize, as well as how to get more nourishment from every sip of water. On several occasions, he has taken care of me emotionally, drawing out my sadness and dispelling my loneliness. Often, he pours joy and love into me.

After a few years, our relationship shifted from teacher-student into a beautiful friendship. I knew that the dynamics of our relationship were changing when Tim started to ask *me* questions. His curiosity is boundless, and his questioning went on for months. Some of his inquiries were simple. *What is a kitchen? Where do cars come from? Why don't I feel a living consciousness in these vehicles? Is there a biological connection with the person inside?* He was astonished to learn that humans produce cars just to get from place to place. I found it challenging, and quite humorous, to try and explain the emotional connection that some of us have to our fancy sports cars, big trucks, and elegant stretch limousines, which Tim sees when weddings are held in the park.

Tim also wanted to know about mobile phones, comparing our use of wireless communication to the mycelium network that the trees in the park use to communicate.

These phones appear with humans quite often and they seem to strongly influence people's emotions, he has relayed to me.

One day when I arrived in the park, Tim asked me, *Do you like my leaves? I'm pretty proud of them.* This caused me to research his species of golden elm and I discovered why he is so proud of his leaf canopy. There's always something more to learn!

Whenever I share the tree wisdom that I've gained, I find myself just saying that I learned this or that from my friend Tim, without disclosing his species. Tim has truly taught me so much about myself.

Be still and shine. When it's quiet, I stand and I focus on just being a tree. I feel the sun, the earth, and me all mixing together.

He coaches me by saying, *When you are still and completely connecting to your unique self, you radiate an incredible amount of love. Watch me.*

Tim has helped me to accept that I am beautiful and loving. In any given moment, I can choose to shine and radiate love. At 100 percent, I feel confident and secure. At 120 percent, I feel powerful, generous, and grateful. At 150 percent, feelings of expansiveness mix with ripples of love that burst out from me in every direction.

This all comes from an inexhaustible internal source of magic. It feels wonderful. It is delicious to just be me, in my full radiance.

Along with his visual shine, the most beautiful sensations of acceptance and love emanate from Tim in tingling waves of unconditional love. As a bonus, he invites me to stand with my back against his trunk. As we merge bodies, we shine together. It is a profound experience. All time and sensation vanish as we become the pure, radiant, shimmering energy of love.

John Paul (Eagle Heart) Fischbach

HEARING EARTH'S VOICE

*T*he sun wanders in and out of the clouds, and the air feels fresh with impending spring. I'm excited to have a free day, since my work as a corporate lawyer is typically a crush of phone calls, emails, paperwork, and frustration. *Should I take my horse out for a ride? Do yardwork? Or round up my husband, Steve, and our big black dog, Q, for a walk on the trails?*

"Well, what should I do today?' I ask aloud to myself while gazing out the window.

That is when the ordinary day became extraordinary. *Take dictation from the Earth,* I hear clairaudiently.

Pivoting in surprise, I know there is no one there. I stand still for a few moments, pondering what had just happened.

That's a profound idea, I ponder, *though I'm not sure I'm qualified.* This request seems more suited to the illustrious and knowledgeable spiritual people of our time, not a lawyer ensconced in mundane matters of business logistics. *Oh heck, I'll give it a try.*

Grabbing a pen and some paper, I head outside to the edge of the woods in our backyard. Not knowing exactly what to do, I sit on a stone for a few minutes. All of a sudden, the dictation starts pouring forth so fast that my hand and mind have a hard time keeping up with it. After writing pages of inspired messages, I am amazed and grateful.

That was my first experience with hearing Earth's voice. Over the ensuing months and years, I continued to periodically do this writing practice. When I do, Earth, the primary speaker, always expresses a distinctly feminine tone with a lovely warmth and lightness. There's a rather musical quality to it.

Some of the dictations seem to come from angelic beings who offer expanded guidance in support of Earth's messages. These beings identify themselves simply as WE. Their collective voice is more serious and sonorous, with a masculine tone. The feeling is of being among very wise professors, who speak in a parlance that is poetically rhythmic and a bit archaic.

Each time I settle in to take the dictation, there are moments of complete stillness when I hear nothing. I sense that this serves the purpose of aligning the frequencies among me, the Earth, and the angelic realm, and merging our energies so that we can communicate verbally.

Like that first time out near the woods in my yard, these dictations initially started in an overwhelming rush. The words flowed so quickly that I had to hurry to take it all down. Sometimes I'd get stuck trying to analyze it, which blocked the process. At one point, with worries hovering in my mind over whether I was getting all the information correctly, my concerns were interrupted by WE:

Do not worry about how the words disconnect or connect, Mary, only listen to and transcribe the stream of higher and collective consciousness as it enters your stream.

Once I became accustomed to taking the dictation, my mind adjusted to working with this higher frequency and it became easier and more fluid. It actually began to feel quite natural, not foreign.

All of this, though, seemed to beg the question: *Why me?*

Eventually, it occurred to me to ask the angelic speakers. Their answer was completely practical: *Because you can, and you are willing.* I was surprised by this because I had never perceived myself in this way, but here I was doing it.

As this experience of taking dictation from the Earth continued to unfold, I realized that the rich and varied information being shared was not just for me, but for everyone. *Those who read these words will connect with the resonance, the vibration, which we send through you as you take this dictation. Know that as you are so doing, you are bringing a vibration into the world that is needed here.*

This awareness set me on a different course beyond my law career. I recognized that Earth and WE were dictating a book for all of us about how to perceive and attune to Earth, nature, and ourselves in a new way. They pointedly said, *Now it is time for humanity to learn to channel your energies in a comprehensive way, joining together in thought and deed, consciously supportive of your planet. This is far, far more important than any of your other daily undertakings on Earth.*

Mary E. McNerney

THE SAMAUMA TREE

The sacred ayahuasca ceremony in the Amazon begins with our host, Pajé Renato, singing and offering gratitude for all beings surrounding us, including a magnificent Samauma tree. It's a beautiful spot just outside of Altamira, Brazil. Before this night, I had participated in hundreds of rituals, but this one is special, as my friend Jost and I would be heading upstream in a couple of days on the Rio Iriri to visit Juma, the *cacique* of the Xipaia tribe.

About four hours into the ceremony, I begin to speak silently to the Samauma tree. Feeling truly grateful for her presence and wisdom, this humble conversation leads us to focus on my right shoulder. I had been feeling pain in it for about two years, and none of the natural therapists I'd seen had been able to resolve it.

Please show me the cause of my shoulder pain and help take it away, I request.

The tree instructs me to lie down in front of her in a fetal position. I stay like this for some time, until I intuit that the tree wants me to get up and stand close to her huge trunk and side roots. The tree is so majestic that her presence feels like having a loving, protective, wooden wall of support to my left and right.

With open palms, I press my left and right hands into the side roots and close my eyes.

I am ready to receive your help.

Suddenly, a bolt of what feels like electricity streams out of the side roots. It shoots through my arms and into my head and feet, down to the middle of the earth, and up into the sky. The shock of it causes me to scream and I try to step back from the trunk, but can't. It's like I am glued to her.

The energy flow continues for about 20 minutes. As it lessens, I'm able to release my hands from the roots. I fall to my knees and lie on the rainforest floor, crying and completely grateful, as there is no doubt that a powerful energy exchange has just taken place. It lulls me into a deep sleep, and I dream beautiful dreams.

Three days later, after sitting in a boat for about 12 hours, I realize that the pain in my right shoulder is gone. Pajé later tells me that he and a friend who lives on the land both saw a black shadow in the form of a *minotauro* leave my body while I was glued to the Samauma.

The pain has never returned, and I remain grateful that the ancient indigenous wisdom of nature has the power to heal the world and all its creatures, including human beings.

Chris Bachmann

WHEN THE FAIRIES APPEARED

Nature has always been a nurturing, abiding companion for me, especially in times of strife. In 2002, I needed that stability more than ever. My marriage of 27 years was coming to an end after a long, rocky haul. Depleted spiritually, I was aching for renewal.

Fortunately, we had recently moved our family of five to a cottage house situated on the edge of an Audubon preserve, a setting that reminded me of my childhood. Being in this natural environment gave me hope and allowed my heart to sing once again.

One evening after dinner, I escaped to the trail behind our house for a solitary sunset walk. There was something magical about this landscape at dusk, when the visitors had gone home and the forest quieted down. It felt like entering another realm, with a gentle fog in the air, deer nibbling on a dinner of shrubbery, and the low light mysteriously illuminating the green plants from within. As I walked through this forest, I felt like an honored guest, and the magic of the Divine seemed to permeate my entire being.

At bedtime after that walk, I fell into a peaceful sleep and, somewhere between dusk and dawn, experienced a vivid dream. In the magnificent green of the forest, an image appeared: a painting of a tree branch holding a bird's nest. Curled up asleep in the nest was a tiny, delicate fairy adorned in a wispy, gauzy garment of pink. Her arms encircled the blue robin eggs, as if to protect them while the parents were away.

Waking up abruptly, this ephemeral image was so burned into my mind that I felt intensely compelled to replicate it. A fairy! My goodness, not a subject I had ever considered painting, but I was able to draw an accurate representation of the dream vision to my satisfaction, and within 24 hours it was done.

This vivid dream prompted me to research fairy art, and inspired me to paint more of them. An English gentleman that I discovered, David Riche, was developing the first ever fairy artist compilation book. I got busy painting. Within just a few weeks, I had uploaded a handful of fairy images onto my website and asked a number of my email contacts to check out my art.

The next morning after uploading the art, I was stunned to see in my inbox an invitation from David Riche to be in his fairy book. This was in the early days of email, and I could hardly believe that my message had somehow found its way across the ocean while I slept! It felt like the fairies had called to me and I was eager to keep listening.

After my divorce was final, the children and I moved to a house on a hilltop away from the woodland trail. As I read more deeply about the relationship between humans and fairies, I wondered why I had never encountered any of them, given my deep connection to nature.

"Why have I not seen you?" I asked out loud, immediately noticing a ball of fear in my stomach. The realization was undeniable: I had not seen them because I was afraid.

If you really want to see them, I reasoned with myself, *you need to move into trust and release any fear of the unknown.*

I'd read how fairies can show themselves in other forms to communicate with humans, including in the form of a dragonfly. After my evening prayer, I sat on my bed and put out a request.

Dear fairies, I want you to know that I'm not afraid. I believe in you. If you want to show yourself to me in any way, I would be truly happy.

The next morning, as I got ready for work, I walked around to the driver's side of my van and sat my hot mug of tea on the hood so I could open the door. Just then, something zoomed around me then stopped to hover right in front of my face. A huge dragonfly! I took a deep breath in disbelief, as it seemed to be looking straight at me. The dragonfly then swooped and circled back to stare right in my eyes once again.

Astonished, I finally managed to say, "Hello! I know who you are! Thank you for coming to visit and showing yourself to me."

Suddenly, my excitement turned to queasiness in the pit of my stomach. With that, the dragonfly flew off.

In the coming months, I routinely spoke to the fairies anytime I was outdoors, calling them back. In my new home, my forest walks became neighborhood strolls. One of the houses that I regularly walked by was like a quaint museum, with a lovely flower garden. I would address the fairies in the garden, and though I couldn't see them, the flowers would begin moving in response to my greeting. I soon discovered that this was the childhood home of Rachel Carson, the renowned author of *Silent Spring*, the book that fueled the environmental movement. Even more unbelievable to me is that the land that our home sits on was also part of the Carson homestead. I couldn't believe it! Surely this was another nudge by the fairies and no coincidence.

Meanwhile, my fairy art was accepted for inclusion in a second book, which connected me with a larger, global group of fairy artists and publishers. I began contemplating the idea of creating a Fairie Festival in my city. Clearly, the fairies had awakened my muse on many levels. As a single parent, I was being pulled in several directions at once, yet I couldn't release the concept of hosting this festival.

One morning, with all of this on my mind, I opened the kitchen door to leave for the office when something zoomed past my face and flew behind the front wheel of my van.

"Please come out," I coaxed the creature. "Don't be afraid. It's okay."

Out flew the dragonfly... and it landed on the top of my foot. As I smiled down at it in wonder, the dragonfly began tapping on the top of my foot, as if to say, *Everything is going to be alright. Don't worry.* It rested on my foot for several minutes as I admired it and spoke softly to it, then it flew away. I knew that I was being comforted and encouraged by the fairies.

The Fairie Festival did come to life and was a great success. Vendors, musicians, and attendees traveled from far and wide to revel in the joy of fairy life for a weekend. I have stayed closely connected to the fairies ever since, and when I get too wrapped up in life, they tap me on the shoulder and remind me to face my fears, create my own magic, and, most of all, to believe.

Linda Varos

GRANDFATHER TREE

For centuries, a sacred circle of ancient redwood trees has stood proudly, guarded by a magnificent ponderosa pine tree. A friend invited me to telepathically visit these ancient trees holding court on another continent through an energy healing session.

Hesitantly, I accept the distant call. Although I have done remote energy work, I'd never considered connecting with a tree. Yet the pull is forceful and I can't ignore the tree's wishes, which feels like a royal decree.

Lighting a candle and closing my eyes, I begin to pray and ground myself, feeling doubtful, a bit awkward, and immensely nervous. As I ask permission to connect with the ponderosa, I hear the wind rustle her needles. She offers her wonderfully purifying and healing pine fragrance, which balances my emotions and expands my heart's intention to connect.

I feel her energy probing mine then allowing me entrance . . . and as majestic as she is, I swear I hear her giggle, prompting me to step inside. Upon entering, I feel safe and embraced by trust and compassion, the way a child walks hand in hand with her grandfather. In fact, the ponderosa tells me through my inner knowing to address the redwood tree as Grandfather Tree.

Goosebumps well up on my skin and warmth spreads through me. Tears come to my eyes. Layers of doubt and insecurity slip off my shoulders as my spirit soars, and I realize that being in the moment without expectation is sufficient to connect with the wonder of these nature beings.

A bird hammers above me, and I notice golden particles of light swirling through the air, filtering through the branches and leaves. Flecks of sun playfully bump shadows away. What a mesmerizing performance of sound and light!

Excitement rushes through me as the air quickens. In my mind's eye, I see a whirling vortex woven from the fabric of my reality. Magically, my image of the world shifts, revealing another layer where elementals choose to live. Fairies! I am giddy with delight.

The fairies adjust my frequencies and instruct me to align my energy with Grandfather Tree by sitting with my back against his trunk and breathing with him. Inhale, exhale, inhale, exhale . . . slower, deeper, calmer . . . heartbeat after heartbeat.

As my roots wend into Mother Earth, I feel nourished by and attuned to a mystical web of communication interlacing through the planet. As I meld my energy with Grandfather Tree, the sun plays upon my leaves and my branches reach into the sky, signaling and receiving Divine messages. A deep rush of the Life Force runs up and down the trunk from roots to canopy.

A sense of belonging, of being exactly where I am supposed to be, fills me with such quietness. All that matters is this profound connection to All is One.

Small critters scurry along the bark, with no apparent interest in me—just acting totally confident in their knowledge of having important things to fulfill. Watching them, I am clearly shown my own rightful place in the grand scheme of events.

The connection intensifies even more as Grandfather Tree begins to show me vision after vision, like an old-fashioned slideshow, of people from long ago placing their offerings and sacrifices at his feet to honor his wisdom and show gratitude. So much laughter and sorrow. I see Grandfather Tree patiently consoling a crying mother who has lost her son. Battles being fought, brother to brother, tribe against tribe, century after century. Animals being birthed or passing over under the umbrella of his peaceful protection. Plant beings taking root, spreading their seeds and other gifts, and returning to the soil.

So much blood, so much happiness. Grandfather Tree has witnessed it all during these centuries, serving as a powerful conduit between Mother Earth and the heavens above.

The visions continue, with faces coming into focus, one after another . . . many overlapping stories and overwhelming emotions. My breath catches and I become a little dizzy trying to keep up with the visions that Tree is revealing to me.

Through it all, I keenly sense his tangible love and compassion for all, his willingness to offer transmuting energy to anyone who is willing to receive it. Never judging, just accepting and absorbing all that has been told to him.

Focusing on the Divine spark within everyone and everything, Tree allows all of these stories, while knowing that the truest story underlying them is rooted in the Divine.

A deep awareness rushes in: We are all one. We are all radiant. Everything that happens serves to bring us back to that Divine inner energy. With this lifting of the veil of density, I consciously feel what I had, until now, forced myself to believe about interconnectedness. Now I know . . . Every time I consciously hurt another sentient being, I hurt myself. When I hurt myself, I hurt all other beings . . . and the echoes of these wounds are felt through all time, layers, and spaces.

Be as conscious as you are able to be. This is Grandfather Tree's parting guidance for me. Now I can go forward, attentively listening to the colors of the wind, the giggles of trees, and spreading gold dust with the fairies.

Part Two

Living within that total freedom of connection and grounded as never before, I close my remote energy session, bubbling with joy, ease, and grace.

Florentine Bisschops

DIVINE CLOUDS

We had been here before. As the car rolled to a stop, I stepped onto the gravel path leading to the water's edge with a sense of wonder and exhilaration. The smell of freshly mown grass was unmistakable, the trees were laden with tightly folded buds on the verge of explosion, and the lake water rippled gently towards the shoreline, bouncing against rocks piled along the boat slips.

A family of ducks bobbed in the current. As if taking turns, their heads suddenly submerged then returned to the surface in search of food. Nearby, a stately blue heron stood motionless in the shadows, while several small birds took off from the forest of trees into the sapphire blue sky.

We stood in silence, as was our custom, until I felt the pulse of Spirit beckoning me to send forth the sacred sounds of singing. As the notes took flight and twirled into the air, the wind strengthened and the waves quickened on the water.

For years, the two of us had been doing what we call land work. Feeling called to certain areas in our county that we intuitively felt needed a charge of positive energy, we would travel there to do prayer work, toning, and singing. We did not always have an exact understanding of what we were working on, and it didn't always feel comfortable, but these heartfelt excursions were our way of helping, and we always sensed a release and a calming of the energy in the area after our sessions.

Before departing for this trip to the lake, I got an overwhelming nudge to take a camera with me, so I popped one into my bag. When we arrived on this cool spring day, the area was abandoned. We felt the need to have our feet touching the water, so we stood at the water's edge, close together with our elbows touching. With our feet wet from the lapping waves, we began our prayer ritual.

As the inspiration arose, each of us would sing a note or do toning. I have several sacred songs, which always give us a great feeling of the presence of the Divine. They start out soft and low, with the melody rising to a crescendo until the last refrain soars in the highest frequency and fullest tones.

As I sang that day and these sacred sounds grew stronger, the wind began to quicken around us and clouds moved in. We watched in awe as their billowy whiteness came into view and formed the shape of what looked like two swans standing face to face with their necks curved, creating a heart shape.

I reached into my coat pocket for my camera, but wasn't quick enough to capture this vision. I continued to sing and send sacred tones into the air. As I did so, another cloud moved into view and suddenly opened to reveal the beautiful profile of an angel. This time, I was quick enough to snap several photos before the formation folded back upon itself and was gone.

Speechless, we looked at each other and raised our arms to the heavens in gratitude for this extraordinary breath of the Divine. When our session was complete, we walked back to the car and discussed what we had just seen and felt. *Were there really swans and an angel sailing across the sky?*

Soon after, I picked up my developed photos from the store and was amazed at the clarity of the angel photos. I made copies and shared them with loved ones. The most beautiful moments were enjoyed when someone would scan the photos and suddenly recognize the angelic profile in the cloud. With wide-eyed surprise, they'd give me a knowing glance of love and gratitude.

The feeling of that incredible day is still in my heart years later . . . and I've given the photo a title: "The heavens are telling the glory of God."

Marian S. Taylor

SPIRIT OF THE WIND

A hint of chill was in the air on a sunny spring day at Bear Paw Meadow. This sacred land high in the remote mountains of north-central California is where a group of us were creating a sustainable community run by solar power.

My project that day was constructing a chicken coop from the ruins of an old log cabin. It's situated at the edge of a fertile meadow, in the shade of a spectacular grandfather oak tree, and adjacent to a muddy bog where water seeps up from the earth. We pump fresh spring water on this spot.

While working on the coop, I noticed that the wind would blow particularly hard in certain areas around the cabin. The cold seemed to pierce right through me. Most of the roof siding had blown off, and the oak tree was growing tall and strong right outside the empty door frame. In this particular spot, the wind always felt downright hostile towards me, like it didn't want me there.

That spring day, it occurred to me that our community was, in a sense, invading this sacred turf, and I hadn't formally asked permission from the spirit of the land. With this awareness, I stood in the doorway, facing the magnificent panoramic view of the mountains to the west, and opened my arms to the sky. Allowing the cold wind to blow hard against me, I began to pray by introducing myself.

"My name is Jack Allis," I said aloud. "I am your humble servant, and a humble servant of this creation. This is something that I know we share. I understand why you feel hostile toward humans. I sincerely apologize for any damage that humanity has inflicted on Mother Earth."

Truly feeling and meaning every word, I asked the natural forces of this land to open a channel through which we could communicate and exchange energies.

"Our community is different, as we are not here to do harm," I explained. "We are a band of humans who remember who we are, and why we are here. We are doing this work in service to Creation, not plundering it. Our desire is to live in harmony again with the forces of nature and with the spirit world."

As I continued this prayer ritual with an open heart and mind, I asked the spirit of the land to join us, become our ally, and guide us in our work. The challenges we faced in creating this community were great, after all, and we needed all of the help we could get. Throughout this ritual, the frigid wind continued to bash me and rip through the branches of the grandfather oak, clattering any old loose metal remaining on the roof.

"What is your name?" I asked upon closing my prayer. Nothing came to me.

"Okay, I'm just going to call you the spirit of the wind that blows through this spot."

When I spoke these words, the wind stopped . . . everything stopped. Suddenly, the atmosphere was breathlessly calm . . . no sound or movement . . . no birds, insects, jets . . . nothing. The entire world seemed to pause for this sacred moment.

As I closed my eyes and breathed deeply, a surge of warmth flowed through me and onto my face. My body felt as light as the air. Rooted to this spot like the great oak standing beside me, time vanished. Peacefulness and joy permeated these moments, both inside of me, and outside.

After a few moments, I opened my eyes, and a gentle puff of warm wind caressed my face through the doorway from the west. Everything briefly went still again, then the wind started to blow like before, just not as intense.

"Thank you." I reached out my arms in acknowledgment of this omen, which was clear as a bell. The spirit of the wind and I now had a relationship. He was my friend, and I would continue to pray to him as we built our community.

A week later, I made a huge fire in the chicken coop area from an immense pile of scrap wood. I asked both the fire and the spirit of the wind for any guidance they might wish to share. I stared into the flames, mesmerized, and was startled to hear a sudden, unfamiliar racket. The metal roof began to rattle uncontrollably, like the sound of an oncoming earthquake.

In the next instant, a huge gust of wind smashed through the empty doorway and knocked me off balance. Fear overtook me as I grabbed a bucket of water to douse the fire, which I was certain would spread due to the intense wind fanning the flames in every direction.

My eyes darted to the fire, expecting to see cinders and pieces of flaming wood wildly blowing around. Surprisingly, the fire was perfectly contained in a neat circle that was now emitting a stupendous glow. The fire rumbled and roared like a blast furnace at the beginning of time.

Completely mesmerized, this ball of light took possession of my consciousness and spirit. I was no longer afraid. I set down the bucket, and while the wind continued to swirl all around, I could no longer feel it. The sensation was similar to calmly watching a scene through a window. In other moments, it was like being in the center of a swirling vortex, with the flames glowing so brightly I had to squint. After a while, this blinding glow was all there was. Time stood still again.

Part Two

Eventually, the wind subsided and I opened my eyes. The atmosphere returned to how it was before, slightly breezy, and the fire was once again just a small bonfire.

Soaking this in for a moment, I heard another rush of ferocious wind rumbling like a cosmic freight train on the other side of the meadow along the mountain slope. The wind had formed a funnel cloud and was vividly swirling through the oak and juniper trees, their branches getting sucked into its violent whirlpool. I watched in awe and with no fear as this little tornado swirled clockwise several times then blew away to the west, returning everything back to calm.

It's clear to me that this was the wind spirit I'd met at the chicken coop. He was revealing how powerful he can be, maybe even showing off a little. Our community is blessed to have the spirit of the wind as our ally . . . and now we can honor this sacred land to the fullest.

Jack Allis

TRINITY AND THE TORNADO

*L*ike the contractions of an overdue pregnant woman, my phone's severe weather alerts grew increasingly frequent, escalating from tornado warnings to watches. Driving home in a ferocious thunderstorm, our thoughts were on the wonderful people my husband, Greg, and I had met at an actor's and writer's workshop in our new hometown of Nashville.

The storm didn't let up as we turned onto our tree-lined street, known for its magnificent, mature oaks and maples. Along our back fence, more trees created a cocoon of privacy. Towering and somewhat grouchy hackberry trees guarded the front. We felt at home in this special spot, only steps away from a fairy forest and miles of protected parklands.

My favorite tree was Trinity, a triple-trunked mulberry that spread her limbs just outside the south-facing windows of my office. On the northern side was another bank of windows where I'd hung a stained-glass version of Trinity. So, she was always around me while I worked and meditated.

Years of a meditation practice may have helped to keep me calm for a while, but by 11 o'clock that night, my anxiety level had begun rising as I

Part Two

continued to track the storm. Greg went to bed as though nothing was wrong; we'd already experienced a number of tornado warnings since moving here three months prior from Wisconsin. When sirens erupted throughout the city and the ear-piercing command to get to a safe shelter roared from every electronic device we owned, I dragged Greg out of bed.

We raced to the unfinished, dingy basement, while blinding flashes of light burst through the house as the city's electric transformers blew out, cutting all power. Before Greg could close the basement door behind him, a powerful burst of wind slammed it shut, almost pushing him down the stairs.

We waited in the dark, listening intently as the sirens and warnings continued... and then... it came. All of the disturbing stories I'd heard about tornados came true, including the sound of a roaring freight train, followed by unnerving silence and extreme changes in air pressure.

Helplessly listening to the thunderous crashes above us for the next few minutes—it's difficult to say exactly how long it lasted—we simply squeezed each other's hands. Glued to my weather app, at 12:40 in the morning, the radar indicated that the tornado had passed over us and moved on.

When we cautiously ventured upstairs, we were relieved to find that our house was still standing, but now the wind was fiercely ripping through every room. All of the windows had shattered, leaving broken glass, debris, and rainwater everywhere.

"We're okay. We're okay. We're okay." We kept saying this to each other.

Armed with flashlights, we surveyed the damage. My office was the worst hit. The desk was buried under a pile of rubble, and Trinity had been uprooted, crashing through the wall of windows.

Walking around in a daze, I glanced up at the ceiling lights in the living and dining rooms, and noticed that they were quickly filling with water. Greg went into the attic to investigate; when he returned, he was as white as a sheet.

"We've got to get out of here!" *But where? And how?* It was too dangerous to go outside, so we stayed in, keeping busy by sweeping up glass and packing a few necessities.

When daylight broke, we ventured outside to survey the damage around our yard and in the neighborhood, carefully stepping over downed power lines and uprooted trees. All of the trees along the fence line, and the fence itself, were gone. We were shocked by the sight of our neighbors' homes, or what was left of them. The tornado had sheared off roofs and exterior walls, creating life-sized dollhouses that exposed bathrooms, bedrooms, clothes closets, and personal possessions.

Magnificent oaks had been uprooted and were now strewn over houses and across the roadways. Power lines were down, trapping us on our street.

In the grief-stricken days that followed, we walked around our community like zombies, trying to comprehend the sheer magnitude of the destruction, and meeting many of our neighbors for the first time. Greg joined a scruffy band of chainsaw-wielding men who freed up our isolated street from the fallen trees. I had hoped that only one part of Trinity had fallen through my office wall; but no, all three of her trunks had been uprooted.

The loss of so many mature trees brought tears to my eyes, as did the sight of hundreds of volunteers—people we'd never met—clearing debris and helping each other. It touched my heart to see small children coming around with wagonfuls of bottled water and Moon Pie snacks. At the nearby fire station, more support arrived: makeshift medical units, volunteer sign-up tables, and power-charging stations for the phones we were now dependent upon. Local restaurants brought in food trucks and handed out free lunches . . . and, of course, local musicians joined together to lift our spirits. This was still Music City, after all.

Our streets became lined with mountains of debris awaiting pickup by enormous trucks that rolled in from Alabama like a fleet of oversized tanks.

The debris mountains offered glimpses of shattered lives: dolls' heads, broken bassinets, fragments of a grandmother's china, all awaiting their trips to the dump. Our once-thriving community was now a bizarre assembly of vacant lots and enormous pits. The homes that remained intact, including ours, had boarded up windows and bright, blue tarps tacked onto their roofs.

Barely two weeks later, the stay-at-home orders for Covid-19 went into effect nationwide. Before we could fully comprehend what was going on, all of the FEMA employees, utility workers, insurance claim reps, and local volunteers were gone. Tornado survivors didn't know whether contractors could secure construction materials to restore our homes, and many families were now homeless.

For the next three months, Greg and I were nomads, venturing from one temporary living quarter to another, practicing the exhausting ritual of sanitizing every surface. When our local newspaper finally published aerial photographs of the storm, we learned that the worst hit area was less than 100 yards behind our home.

That's when it dawned on me: The trees surrounding our home had served as a buffer. Tears came to my eyes as I realized that they had sacrificed themselves for our protection. And on an even more personal level, it came into my awareness that by crashing through my office—which was, unwittingly, sort of a memorial to my previous achievements—Trinity was telling me to be present and create my new future.

As the months passed, we all began the process of reconstruction and healing. Nonprofit groups formed to help replace the tree canopy around our yard. The fairy forest and park had suffered tremendous losses. Before city services grinded to a halt, the Parks Department crews made attempts to cut down some of the more severely damaged trees, but several were left in mid-saw, slashed and left for dead. They were deformed and split through their hearts... and I loved them. I put my hands on them and talked to them.

On one of my neighborhood walks, I approached a lovely oak tree whom I'd never spoken to before. She appeared completely undamaged. Feeling drawn to her, I aligned my spine with her thick trunk, fully embraced her, then went into a kind of trance, completely reliving what she experienced during the tornado... the winds, the hail, all of it. And she stood solid, stoic, and unyielding... taking it all, never complaining or grieving.

She helped me to remember what I'd known all along about the damage we sustained to our private property because of the tornado: It wasn't personal! The tornado didn't single out me, or Greg, or our neighbors. Our human narcissism made us feel like victims, but Nature had to do what Nature had to do.

Countless miracles continued to reveal themselves. The stained-glass version of Trinity survived with only a tiny crack, even though the window she'd hung in was completely blown out. And when Greg took his chainsaw to Trinity's broken limbs, they sliced apart into perfect heart-shaped pieces, which now hang in spaces around our yard in her honor.

In the two years since the tornado, we've planted more than 20 young trees in our yard. Where our buffer trees once stood lies a swath of 44 bamboos, providing a green border to soften the sight of towering new edifices that have sprung up in our booming city. Each day, more buildings rise around us, overlooking the yard that we are filling with vegetable gardens and honeysuckle vines for the pollinators.

Nowadays, I awaken at four o'clock in the morning and venture out into the stillness. At the medicine wheel, where Trinity once blessed us with her presence, I invoke the four directions. I touch each tender tree and bamboo culm, offering thanks and encouragement. And before the onslaught of trucks and construction workers start their day, I practice qi gong, ending with a grounding exercise, called "bamboo in the wind." I connect to Mother Earth below and Father Sky above.

Part Two

Every day, the bamboo is teaching me to be flexible and to weather the storms of life. We still get weather alerts fairly often in Nashville. When we do, I remember the trees that so lovingly shielded us, and my dear Trinity . . . and I become a bamboo in the wind.

Brooke Maroldi

REDWOOD FAMILY AND BLISS TREE

I met my five redwood trees when I moved to Mill Valley, California to teach at a Waldorf-inspired school. The backyard of the cottage house I'd arranged to rent, sight unseen, felt like a small forest with these 100-foot redwoods.

Every day, I'd touch the bark of each tree and say, "I love you." I gave them all names: Big Red, Sweet Red, Sister Red, Pretty Red, and Brother Red, as each had a unique personality.

When I stood with my back against the trunk of Big Red, the redwood tree elder, I felt calm, strength, support, and love.

Sweet Red had a loving, gentle presence and while sitting near her, listening to the nearby creek, and breathing slowly and deeply, I learned to meditate. I'd sit next to Sweet Red while taking meals and reading books. A hummingbird often came to drink the nectar of nearby wild, red flowers. On the tiny saplings that grew around Sweet Red and the other trees, I'd see small spiderwebs with morning dewdrops. Squirrels would jump and chase especially around Big Red and up his branches.

Pretty Red, at first, seemed angry about how the human landlords of this property had treated the trees. She didn't like the way all her lower branches had been trimmed. Her energy is very strong, making it hard for me to spend too much time with her. A friend of mine who is a therapist came to visit one day, and upon introducing her to my circle of trees, she made a special connection with Pretty Red and spent a long time with her. After that, I received Pretty Red's trust and she was more receptive to my hugs.

Brother Red had a lovely energy, but for a long time, I wasn't able to connect with him. One day, while teaching children's reiki to an eight-year-old boy, he wanted to sit next to Brother Red and send reiki to him. Upon doing that, I could feel Brother Red's energy as gentle, loving, and masculine.

Sister Red was closest to the neighbor's property line and wanted to be included in my morning greetings. One afternoon, my second-grade students came to my cottage for a picnic. They were introduced to the redwoods and I showed them how I greeted each tree. They all chose their favorite tree and spent time with them.

After two years in California, it was time for us to move back to Oregon. As I was packing up and went outside to say goodbye to the redwoods, I felt all five Tree Spirits step forward, like tall light beings. They formed a circle around me and embraced me. In awe and amazement, and filled with joy, ecstasy, and love, I felt humbled and honored to be accepted as a part of this tree circle.

It was difficult to say goodbye to them, as they felt like my family and I didn't know if I would be able to see them again.

When I moved back to Oregon, I began to visit a ponderosa pine that I called my Bliss Tree. She lives in a park by the Deschutes River, and I continued to learn about meditation sitting with her. When I breathe deeply, my energy flows from the top of my head through my body, and merges with Bliss Tree as we travel into Mother Earth. We are received with love by Gaia, and we travel back up through my body and Bliss Tree's trunk. This love frequency feels even more amplified when I sit with my back next to her.

It is Bliss Tree who helped me reconnect with my dear California redwoods. With her help and with long-distance reiki, we are able to journey to my redwoods for visits. When we do so, Bliss Tree sends us through her energy roots as I send reiki, and together, we connect with Big Red and Sweet Red.

When we arrive, I can almost hear them say, *She's here* . . . and they gather to greet us in a loving energetic embrace, like beloved family members welcoming me back home.

Jyoti Noel

THE SACRED STONES

"The stones want to speak to you," my friend, Helen, messaged.

I knew immediately what stones she was referring to because I'd carried them in my heart since the previous summer when I stood beside them and breathed in the timelessness of their wisdom. While visiting Helen and her herd of horses at her sanctuary, The Haven, in Greenfield, England, each day I was drawn to a large stone formation at the top of a distant hill. Knowing that I was being compelled towards it, I asked Helen what it was.

"That's Pots and Pans, an ancient Druid site."

"Can we go there? I'd really like to visit."

"Yes. It's a climb, but I'm happy to take you."

The next day, we set out on a hike up the beautiful English countryside. Walking among the wildflowers that dotted the lush green fields, Helen, her dog, Boi, and I passed sheep and goats peacefully grazing with their lambs and kids playing nearby. When we reached the plateau, the 360° view was breathtaking. With a clear sky the color of cornflowers, we could see for miles across the valley, the large stream cutting through, and the nearby hills.

Part Two

Taking it all in, we approached Pots and Pans and I noticed that this natural formation had large, bowl-shaped indentations worn into the top.

"They're known locally as the Druid Stones," Helen shared. "Local legend states that the bowls hold magical properties. Water collected from them is said to cure eye problems."

As Helen spoke, *my* eyes caught sight of an even larger stone formation further up the hill. We continued our trek and the closer we got to this natural structure, the more I could feel its powerful energy.

Once we reached the summit, I could see two large outcroppings of rocks, seemingly matching in size and shape, standing opposite of each other, forming a center walkway. On each end, faces of guardian spirits were visible in the stones. I could envision this massive formation being used by the Druids for ceremony, walking in procession through this majestic stone doorway leading downhill to Pots and Pans.

Turning my face to the shining sun, I leaned against the cool stones and breathed. Time stood still as I felt everything and nothing at once. Eons of wisdom, stories, and emotions filled the void. Feeling immense gratitude and reciprocity, I pulled down the golden Light from above until it suffused me, the stones, and the sacred land we stood upon in a sharing of Divine love.

I remembered this glorious experience at the Druid site in England as I read Helen's message and was intrigued and excited to learn that the stones remembered me. Knowing that this call to speak with them was an honor, the next morning I gave thanks and entered a meditation with the intention of connecting.

As I closed my eyes, the vision began. Breathing deeply, I was once again on the hillside in England. This time, when I leaned against the stones and turned towards the sun, my body began to dematerialize. Simultaneously, I watched and experienced my physical being crystalize into light and become absorbed by the formation. I wasn't afraid, as I knew that to hear the stones, I needed to be the stones.

And I was.

The stones transported me around the world, showing me current, well-known sacred sites and smaller, less known stone structures. With each new vision, they communicated the critical need to not only reenergize the land at these sites with the frequency of Divine love, but to reconnect the energies of sacred stone sites around the world. They communicated: *These stone formations are an energetic network that is critical to the health of the Earth and all her inhabitants.*

Along with Uluru in Australia, the pyramids in Egypt, Stonehenge and Avebury in England, Mt. Fuji in Japan, Sedona in the United States, and others, they revealed to me the large rock face in the backyard of my previous home. *The larger, well-known sites are important, yet so are the countless other stone formations that you may not pay attention to. They, too, are important connections along the energy grid.*

You are to be a part of this work, bringing Divine light through you and as you. Sharing with the natural world is an important part of the process . . . so is reverence and gratitude for all the seen and unseen sentient beings that you share the world with.

Completing the meditation, I was content with not yet understanding how I would be serving, or who the others were. Upon opening my eyes, I was filled with a knowing that more was to come and, for now, my awareness of this sacred work was enough.

Since then, I have learned that my vision was similar to one that has been imparted to certain indigenous elders around the world. Reenergizing sacred sites is an important piece of the global work they have been doing to restore balance and health to our planet.

Part Two

My part is still unfolding . . . although, as I write this, the stones are speaking again, granting me permission to share my profound experience with all of you. In doing so, I smile in knowing that our circle of sentient beings who walk with reverence on our earth is ever growing.

Rev. Ariel Patricia

A LIFE CHANGING QUEST

The alarm clock sounded its early morning song and I sat up with a jolt. This was the day for me to be taken high up into Carson Forest and left there alone to experience my first vision quest. Admittedly, I was nervous, excited, and terrified that I might be attacked by a mountain cat or wolf, or worse still, bitten by a snake.

I dressed comfortably and headed down to the meeting area where a guide was waiting to lead me to the sweat lodge, so the shaman could purify my energy field. The gentle shaman invited me to enter the lodge and sit on the opposite side of the fire. Another staff member, using deer antlers, delivered stones for the fire. Beautiful, soft music played as we waited for the stones to heat. Eventually, the shaman began to chant a powerful prayer for the success of my quest.

When the flap was opened, two people were waiting to take me into the forest. I carried with me a small pack containing jars of tobacco and dried lavender to be used to create a sacred circle, where I would sit and await Spirit's answer or wisdom. After reaching my drop off point, my escorts wished me success and said they would know when to come back for me, either that day or the next morning.

Glancing around to feel the energy in the forest, I hoped to intuitively know which way to go and make my circle. As a city girl who grew up in the center of Dublin, the silence was different than anything I'd ever experienced. Here, the trees were bigger than any I'd seen in Ireland, and the density and fragrance of the flora was spellbinding.

Spotting a mound of moss, I decided that one of them would be my bed for the night, and a nearby clearing would be the perfect spot to set up my sacred circle. Opening the jars of tobacco and lavender, I closed my eyes and said a prayer to Spirit. Surprised at how calm I felt, I asked for guidance regarding a difficult life decision that I needed to make.

After some time, a chipmunk came out to see who this human visitor was in the forest.

"Good morning! It's lovely to see you," I said. "My name is Patrishe."

He took off fast then returned a few moments later with a friend.

"Good morning," I repeated. "I mean you no harm. I am here to speak with Spirit."

They were gone again in seconds, and I found myself laughing and feeling happy in my heart. All was quiet as the sun began to rise and warm the air.

"Good morning, Sun," I spoke in greeting. "Thank you for this lovely morning and the gift of your warmth."

Feeling safe and comfortable, I began a meditation. After sitting for a while, I heard the sound of a bird determined to get my attention. Opening my eyes just for a moment, I looked around and spotted a red-breasted hummingbird at the top of a very large tree.

"Hello! You are beautiful!" I complimented him.

At the sound of my voice, he left his perch and flew toward me so fast that I thought he was going to crash into my face. Just as he got close, he slowed down and hovered for a couple of seconds in front of me... then flew around my head twice, each time his silk feathers brushing my cheeks. It was an exquisite feeling, like being stroked by the finest silk.

The hummingbird began spiraling down my body all the way to my ankles. Once there, he circled my ankles twice before flying up to hover in front of my third eye. Magically, he spoke into my third eye for what seemed like a very long time. How I wished I understood Hummingbird language! After a while, he flew back up into the tree yet continued to speak to me. Finally, the bird circled above me three times and flew away.

Pure love and awe filled my heart as Spirit, in the form of a beautiful hummingbird, had come to answer my quest. Even though I did not understand the message at that time, I knew instinctively that it involved a descent to the lower worlds as part of my spiritual awakening to wholeness.

Around 10 o'clock in the morning, I remembered the moss mound and decided to lie down for a while. Stretching out in the sun and the precious, silent energy of the forest, my eyes feasted on the beauty and majesty of the trees towering around me. With deep admiration, I found myself wondering how old they were.

At that moment, I made a statement out loud: "I wonder what it is like to be a tree."

To my amazement, within seconds, I found myself inside Tree consciousness, a collective consciousness that is incredibly alive and in communion with everything around it. I indeed got to experience what it's like to be a tree!

At some point, a fly landed on me, and as Tree, I loved it. I told the fly how happy I was that it came to visit me. As Tree, I saw its lovely legs, the shine in its eyes, the rainbows in its wings. As Tree, I knew that fly.

As Patrishe, in that moment, I knew I would never hurt a fly again. I became aware of the tiny creatures on the ground working diligently to break up the small pieces of wood and debris on the forest floor, recycling it all back to the earth. Such perfect order. Everyone knew their task and did it wholeheartedly. No complaining.

Part Two

The next gift in this quest was the arrival of a large wasp, an insect that I had always been nervous and jumpy around. Now, as Tree, I was looking at the most beautiful creation. I could see that its yellow-and-black appearance was actually comprised of hundreds of the finest, silkiest threads weaving together in an intricate pattern to form its coat.

As Tree, I loved them both with all of my being, the fly and the wasp.

At some point, I found myself back on the mossy mound. About seven hours had passed since I had begun my experience with Tree consciousness. Wow! It seemed like mere minutes.

Soon, I heard the vehicle and the voices calling my name so I trudged to the meeting point, but not before saying goodbye to my new forest friends.

Since that trip, I talk to the flies and bees and other creatures that cross my path every day. While out walking my dog, I stop, touch and connect with a tree or two or three along the way. Experiencing nature up close and personal has made such a difference in my life, as I now know I am one with it.

Patrishe Maxwell

A TALE OF TWO TREES

The house sat on a magical strip of land with a cascading creek flowing gently before it. Tall evergreens towered above and around the house, as if holding it in a gentle embrace. The moment I first caught sight of how the trees gave way to a magnificent view, it took my breath away and made my soul rejoice. I'd found my forever home.

To the east was an untamed ravine. To the south, an emerald forest of cedars and Douglas firs. To the west, immature cottonwoods vied for a view of the lake. To the north, the meandering creek was overshadowed by more cedar, fir, and hemlock trees for as high as the eye could see.

My bond with the trees was inevitable and their constant presence undeniable. Tall and strong, they watched over me at every turn, keeping me safe. One tree, in particular, stood out from all the others. I call her Cedarfriend, a beautiful red cedar within full view of the split staircase leading to the second level. The windows follow her statuesque trunk stretching forever skyward.

The base of her trunk caught my eye and concern, though. Strong roots reached out in all directions, with soft, sandy soil spilling all around them. As time progressed and the soil shifted, as soil often does, a large opening between these vast roots and her trunk was exposed. Each glance while walking up or down the staircase towards Cedarfriend was a reminder of this vulnerability. Thus began our daily conversations.

Like many children of my generation, days were spent climbing trees. Talking to trees and animals and rocks and everything in between was commonplace, but having them understand, let alone talk back, was a whole different story. My standard practice with Cedarfriend was to remind her, with each and every passing, to stand tall and strong and please keep us safe. Day after day, night after night, my mantra began to sound like a broken record. That is, until one day, Cedarfriend had finally had enough.

This memorable day began as all others, but chores were on the agenda. With laundry neatly folded and balancing upon both arms, I turned onto the landing between the two levels of stairs, gave my friend a loving glance, and recited my worn-out mantra, *Stand tall and strong and please keep us safe*, without a thought, like I had done a thousand times before.

The instant the words left my lips, I heard loud and clear, as if someone was standing next to me and beckoning in my ear, *Enough already! I know what my job is! Stop telling me!* Shock filtered throughout my body, causing my toe to abruptly catch the lip of the stair, forcing all things upright to come crashing down. As I lay in the heap of clothes scattered about the stairs, my mind was aflush.

What? Was that really . . . the tree?

Sitting on the stairs, I looked at Cedarfriend in bewilderment. I had just gotten yelled at—yes, yelled at—by a *tree*.

As that reality settled in, I chucked and said joyfully, "So you have been hearing me all these years. What do you know?"

Twenty-plus years later, our strong friendship and mutual understanding continues, as Cedarfriend continues to teach me that, yes, humans and trees can communicate. This awareness has led to a profound connection of turning to the trees for guidance, comfort, and inspiration.

During those years, my husband and I were looking to experience island life, and we decided to purchase a summer home on Orcas Island—the largest of the San Juan Islands situated in the northwestern corner of Washington state, surrounded by the wild Salish Sea. It is a solid piece of rock home to some of the few remaining old-growth forests in the lower 48, with trees that have lived 300+ years, withstanding harsh winter winds and century-old fires.

One day, we found ourselves in a quandary over two houses. The yellow charmer was a quaint and cozy house which sat upon a hill on a small piece of land. From high above it overlooked a popular resort and marina offering a spectacular view of the harbor and the distant islands. The other, older gray one lacked the curb appeal of the yellow charmer, but overlooked a bay, with dazzling orange and gold sunsets. This house also shared space with a handful of old-growth Douglas fir trees that withstood the test of time, sporting broken limbs from storms gone by and blackened scars stretching the length of their trunks from fires long past. It was nearly impossible to not feel an immediate connection to these trees, as their life-force energy was as strong as their mighty trunks.

Minutes progressed to hours as we contemplated our decision. As the sun began to fade, I sat alone beside one of the firs at the base of the gray wooden deck overlooking the bay. As is proper when sharing space, I introduced myself to the tree and began explaining my dilemma. As we sat in silence taking in the wonder of the ancient rocks and trees that surrounded us, I suddenly heard a gentle yet firm voice drift through my head saying, *Please purchase this home as I am lonely and would welcome your company.*

I received this information as if it was commonplace, two beings having a conversation in which one is hoping to receive advice from the other. I casually glanced to the right towards this massive tree which boasted a tempo as calm and steady as a distinguished gentleman and said, "Okay. I would be honored to keep your company."

Part Two

Decision made. Now . . . how to explain my reasoning to my husband. Over the many years of marriage, he had become a bit more open-minded or perhaps somewhat used to my magical encounters with nature, but he himself had not had the pleasure of having a tree talk to him.

As I told my husband of my decision, he asked, "Really? Why this gray house?"

And with that question there was nothing left to do but reveal the conversation between this majestic tree watching over us and myself. Without skipping a beat, he wholeheartedly agreed with honoring the request from such a powerful tree and the decision was made. We purchased the gray house, and upon our arrival, the first thing we did was go out onto the deck and say hello.

As with many things in life, change was on the horizon and nine years later, the time had come to sell the house. I made it abundantly clear to the real estate agent that whoever purchased the house had to have an affinity for the trees that called this property home. After three months, the call came.

"You are not going to believe this!" our relator said in a surprising tone. "I brought a couple to view the house and the moment we stepped out of the car, they asked if I would mind if they walked the property to spend some time with the trees."

I knew then and there that the trees would seal the deal, and that my beautiful tree friend had found another couple who would promise to keep him company.

So much is owed to these wonderful teachers, for they opened my heart and soul to the unlimited possibilities around us. It may seem odd that a tree can be lonely or can have a tolerance limit, but what may be odd to one is just another wondrous day in this magical world we call Life for those that truly connect with the natural world.

Karen B. Shea

SHASTA AND THE PLATONIC SOLIDS

*A*fter a recent divorce, my soul was in need of a supreme intervention and weary bones needed a vacation somewhere in nature. *Ah ha*, I thought, *Mount Shasta!* I had never been there and as I allowed my intuition to lead the way, Spirit guided every step of the planning. With my bags packed, I was on my way to refuel my exhausted body and gain back the confidence I'd lost.

Arriving in Shasta, I rented a car and began the journey, which danced and flowed in an amazing way from the very start. Part of me was happy and carefree, while another part of me wondered why I felt so profoundly connected to every aspect of this experience—even to the rental car, as I'd had thoughts of buying one just like it.

As I twisted and turned throughout the roads of California, it was as if the car was driving itself. The environment seemed unusually etheric and dreamlike; the colors surrounding me were vivid, pristine, and prism like. Everything was perfect, like a painting, and I kept admiring it in disbelief. There was an energy penetrating me, for which I had no name, although I knew I was not my usual self.

Part Two

In an instant, towards the distant mountain, Spirit elicited an infinity sign. In my mind, I heard music that had a wind chime tone to it. My attention was high. To make things even more profound, each car that passed had the quality of a sacred geometric structure. It was evident that Source and I were having our own intimate conversation.

I arrived at Shasta and the hotel. Mt. Shasta is known for its quaint town and vortex energies, and I was passionate about exploring this unusual place. Yet tired from the long flight and so much swirling energy, I decided to pace myself and rest, knowing it would all be there for me later. So, I eased into the rest of the day, still wondering about this supreme essence that was guiding me.

The next morning while sightseeing, I was drawn to a gem store where I quickly fell in love with a Platonic solid set that was on sale. *I have to have these*, I thought, so I bought them. I didn't know much about them, but I was eager to learn and explore.

Wanting them to be close to me, I immediately put them in my pants pocket and felt a quick sense of security. I liked this feeling... until something changed. Suddenly, I became a little faint and heard a crackling sound in my head. Not sure what it was, I just kept walking, still holding the Platonic solids tightly in my hands through my pockets. My steps became smaller and though curious, I was not worried.

Within an instant, the cracking began to sound like fuzzy radio stations in my head. It did not hurt and a euphoric sensation came over me. I was aware and calm but this was something very new to me, so I decided to sit down and return to a balanced state. To my surprise, I couldn't. I sat on a rock and began seeing things at full speed. Images were emerging, shapes were coming and going, subtle colors were spinning, and my state became blissful. I sat quietly with myself and fully took in the experience.

As the energy and shapes subsided, things came into focus. Dangling like a wind chime and spread wide like a 30-foot, accordion-like fabric, a hundred tubes of light were in front of me. They took the shape of paper towel rolls, but were clear, long, and linear. Some looked like icicles with crystals and an edge-like texture. The sight was magical, and I was instructed by my higher self to grab them. Eagerly, I reached out and took hold.

The first one I grabbed had no texture or feel, but I knew I was holding it because I could see it in my hand. It had been communicating with me in an unusual way, as if it were in my head yet speaking to my heart. The lit tube showed a story of my life and how to resolve the unbalanced and unhealthy parts of it. Completely intrigued, I quietly absorbed all of this information.

As the history of this story cleared, I returned the tube and reached for another. The same experience happened. I sensed it was there for me to touch and hold, and when I did, it was a complete expression of me and my past. The second tube held another story of my life and showed multiple ways to let go and achieve positive results.

One by one, as I pulled more tubes close to me, they revealed numerous stories of my life and how to resolve fear and conflict. Childhood experiences that had left me feeling hurt and abandoned, chronic illness, and financial difficulties all seemed to be finding resolutions. Many patterns of belief simply disappeared as I clarified how to proceed with my life.

This mystical experience went on the entire time I was visiting Shasta. The tubes were right there in front of me to grab hold of and explore. As the various tubes left me, the pain of past destructive and karmic patterns dissolved, with music and sacred geometry taking shape. I internalized these shapes and was able to incorporate them into my aura, sound body, breath, and consciousness.

At times, I would close my eyes and become this magnetic force field of light. I was able to hear beyond normal capacity, listening to the vibrations of Mount Shasta. I communicated with rocks and water, fish and ants. It was quite a fulfilling, expansive way to meet the universe and all its brilliance.

Part Two

As I journeyed home, I knew that I would never be the same person or view the world in the same way. I was somewhat overwhelmed and even afraid to accept this new me: more carefree and open to letting go, and trusting the universe and its Divine intervention. I knew I had to honor this teaching and respect all that was shown to me.

Tamara Knox

TREE INITIATION

Exiting my apartment to go for a jaunt in Fort Tryon Park along the Hudson River, I was surprised to feel a spot of sadness in my heart. Not able to pinpoint any immediate reason for it, I simply held the emotion lightly with curiosity and compassion, confident that a walk in this scenic neighborhood park would set me right.

Fort Tryon's plants, animals, and rocks had held me for the past 12 years. They had witnessed me at my happiest and most bereaved, and I felt so blessed that in the concrete jungle of New York City, I had managed to find a marvelous green haven to teach me so much about birds and plants, and how to notice them.

I started down the main path of the famed Heather Garden with my heart full of love and gratitude, when a question came to my tongue. "Who am I?" Immediately, a hawk flew across the sky at an unusually fast speed. I feel a special connection to birds and I watch for augurs, but I wasn't sure if that one had been for me. So, I asked again, "Who am I?"

Once more, the response was instantaneous. Another hawk appeared overhead, then just as suddenly, it stopped in mid-air. I thought it would swoop into the river for a meal, but it continued to hover, as if to say, *Hi, I see you! Do you see me?* When I acknowledged its message, it continued on its way.

At that point, I was positively elated, so I pulled that twirling move that Maria does from *The Sound of Music* when she feels the hills come alive. In the distance, I caught sight of an elm tree that I'd walked by hundreds of times. I tend to have a lot of favorite trees, but I can't say that I'd ever felt particularly connected to *this* tree, in spite of its notable size and location. Yet it seemed to beckon me, and so I found a convenient spot of empty ground to stand on and cozied myself up to its trunk, as if leaning against an old friend. I wondered if I could talk to it, or if it was asleep on account of its barren branches.

As these thoughts went through my mind, my heart was operating on its own wisdom. Positioning myself beside the tree, my heart dropped an anchor into safe harbor. I felt it engage and expand, and I experienced myself in the presence of a much larger heart field. Waves of energy pulsed all around my physical being, similar to receiving a reiki healing. Whatever had been lurking in my heart suddenly surfaced in the form of tears. With a sort of animal knowing, I understood that the tree was helping me release an ancient sorrow.

Struggling to find words for such a visceral experience, it would not be a lie to say that a huge weight was lifted, but this didn't occur in a split second. It felt more like the slow thawing of a massive glacier through the warmth of gentleness and loving kindness. And as those icy layers started to melt, I gradually became aware of a kernel of ancient wisdom that had been confined and forgotten in a distant corner of my soul. With the help of Tree, that buried memory was able to dislodge itself from its frozen prison. It washed its primeval knowing over all levels of my being and seeped into every cell of my body. And I knew a simple truth: I exist, along and in connection with everything else in creation, in an ocean of Love.

How else could I have explained the implausibility of Tree's love for me? How humbling to realize that I had walked past it day after day, year after year, yet in one encounter it showed me that it perceived *exactly* who I was and what I needed with much more clarity than I myself had, and it stepped forward to help.

I have since learned from teachers who work with plant consciousness that the Green People are our elders, and one of their roles is to show us how to become spiritually mature human beings. Yet on that day, without any conceptual frame for what I was experiencing, it felt like I had stepped into a miracle. Upon losing the persistent, irrational sense of loneliness I'd carried within for what felt like lifetimes, I saw myself taking my place at the table of Creation. My tears of sorrow turned to tears of pure joy. My longest-held prayer—a prayer I could never quite put to words, but held deeply in my heart—had finally been answered, and I stumbled around the park laughing for no communicable reason.

After that morning, I devoted myself to visiting Tree regularly for a period of about a month, with the intention of building a relationship with it as I would with a new friend. Although I had taken a tree communication class in the past, to me that kind of engagement always felt forced. I didn't demand any words from Tree. Sometimes I chatted shyly with it just to share bits of my day, but mostly I practiced sending it love and seeing what it wanted to share back. What I enjoyed most was simply standing in silence and breathing with Tree. It taught me that its exhalations formed my inhalations, and that conversely, it breathed in what I breathed out. I spent much of that winter sharing one breath and one heartbeat with Tree.

Every encounter had the possibility of being completely different from the last, and I quickly learned that if I loaded the experience with expectation, I could be sorely disappointed. There were days when all I did was greet Tree and thank it for its friendship, and if I didn't feel any significant outflowing of energy, I would leave it at that. I learned to respect Tree's space by sensing when the field between us would close, and take that as my sign to say goodbye. One such time I started to take my leave, when I suddenly felt my feet stuck in place and my legs get stiff and solid, as if I no longer had knees. I realized that Tree was showing me what it felt like to be rooted into the ground.

Tree also taught me to listen to its call from afar. Both the park and my apartment lay just one block from the train station in opposite directions. If I emerged from the train and felt the pull to go right, I knew that I was to go to the park rather than turn left to head home. I also learned to hear Tree's call in the very first moments of my day.

One such time, Tree woke me and filled me with the inspiration for an early morning visit. I sat on the stone wall behind it to see if I could sense its field without making any physical contact, and I was thrilled to notice that I could feel its energy make its way to my feet, through my legs, and eventually all the way up my body. It compelled me to move closer still, and eventually I made my way to my usual leaning position. First, I felt Tree embrace me like a wise and loving grandparent. But then the embrace grew so engulfing I had to open my eyes to make sure I still had arms and hands. I felt my core merge with the tree trunk to the point of being immobile.

The more I learned what it felt like to be a tree, the more the wounded human parts in me healed, and the more easily I remembered that I belong to the wildness of the world.

Ysette Roces Guevara, Ph.D.

SURRENDERING TO FREEDOM

"This is going to be great!" I exclaimed to my group of fellow tourists in Costa Rica. "I'm so excited!"

Contrary to my announcement, I was not looking forward to the day's whitewater rafting expedition. While I've always loved being in the solace of nature, I'm not a thrill-seeker.

As our group of adventurers huddled around the local guide for a safety lecture, my attention was split between listening to his instructions and fighting my inner world of two competing voices. *Pay attention to everything the guide says. We gotta know the rules. Come on, we've gone rafting before. Nothing bad is gonna happen. Don't be such a downer.* Since leaving home for college, I had been committed to moving beyond the tiny comfort zone I had carefully cultivated as a child, and pushing past the confining fear that governed most of my childhood.

Walking over to a large, lush tree, I silently asked for its help in feeling grounded, reassured, and safe. The tree's energy was distant and unreachable, as if he and his brethren spoke a language I couldn't understand. Uncomforted, something worrisome stirred deep within me. The tense, humid air and overcast skies hinted at the possibility of an incoming storm.

Once the safety lecture concluded, the group broke into smaller sections and we headed to the river. Upon reaching the green and turbulent water, saturated with silt and dirt carried down from the mountains in the recent rains, a spike of worry ran through me. I had honed the skill of pushing aside unpleasant feelings after nearly 20 years of living with a family who seemed more focused on surface-level pleasantries than the depths of any situation. Yet today, with them alongside me on this trip, I struggled to stave off these feelings.

Six people plus a skilled guide would be steering each of the small rafts through the rapids. I took a seat on the left side of the green, inflatable raft behind my father and sister. My mother and two strangers took up corresponding spots on the other side, and our guide positioned himself at the back. As instructed, I securely tucked my right foot into the safety strap on the floor of the vessel, and we pushed offshore.

We bobbed and torqued our way down the first few sets of currents. Splashes of water flew up from random directions and doused us with each twist and drop. A steady hum of unsettledness intensified to a palpable anxiety as we navigated a more agitated portion of the river. Jolts of adrenaline buzzed through my veins each time we'd climb over a swell and crash back down onto the water's surface.

I scrambled to manage all of the competing priorities: maintain a balanced sitting position, keep a solid grip on my paddle, hear and heed the instructions of our guide over the roar of the rapids, and withstand the pulls of gravity and unpredictable splashes.

Amidst the chaos of a turbulent set of rapids, my foot came loose from the safety strap, the only thing securing me to the raft. *Put your foot back in the strap! That's the rule! It's the safety protocol!* The other part of me said the opposite. *Oh, loosen up. Let's have some more fun!*

My dad turned to see how I was doing. I offered up one of my patent *I'm having fun!* fake smiles. For years, those toothy grins had faithfully appeased others and myself. This time, not only did it fail at its job, but the house of cards that had held up my entire outward facade collapsed from the smile's outright falseness. Where that rickety structure once stood was now a chasm of darkness, leaving nothing for me to anchor into.

The next portion of the river was comparatively calm, offering me an opportunity to steady myself and relieve my building worry. With the gaping hollowness inside, my attempts to find any modicum of grounding were fruitless.

Up ahead, the left riverbank jutted out at a sharp angle, creating an eddy in front of it. Our guide worked vigorously to steer us to the right and keep us in the main body of the river. His efforts were unsuccessful, and we were pulled into the swirling waters. I braced the side of the raft as he barked orders to keep us steady and position us to exit the vortex as quickly as possible.

Before we had completed one full revolution around the eddy, centrifugal force pulled me backwards over the lip of the raft, and I splashed down into the cool water.

1 ... 2 ... 3 ... I counted as I had been instructed in the safety lecture, expecting to resurface upon reaching 5 . . . *See? This is why we listen to and follow the rules! Quit worrying! We're fine. This is us having a fun adventure.*

After completing the count, I was still submerged. Confused at the mismatch between expectation and reality, I furiously kept counting. My anxiety inched upwards with each number 6 . . . 7 . . . 8 . . .

When I reached 9, my head broke through the surface tension of the water, offering a brief respite for my fraying nerves. Taking in a breath of air and surveying the scene, I noticed that I had resurfaced 30 feet away from my raft, on the opposite side of the churning eddy.

Knowing the raft was too far for me to swim to safely, I spun around and spotted a large rock near the shore about 10 feet away. Swimming towards it, confident in the strength of my 20-year-old frame, I got within five feet of the rock when the water spiraled around my right leg and pulled me down sharply under the surface.

The shock of being pulled down against my will was disorienting. My anxiety sharpened into fear. With even greater intensity, I resumed swimming in the direction I presumed to be going toward, though with my eyes tightly closed, I wasn't sure which way I was headed.

Reaching and kicking with all my might, I watched for any sign that I was nearing the surface. I looked for the water pressure to lessen, the above-water sounds to become audible, or the brightness of day to penetrate the dark. After aggressively pumping my arms and legs for some time, my energy reserves were nearing empty. My lungs cried out for fresh oxygen. Yet I still saw no indication that my efforts were bringing me to shallower waters.

Discouraged and fatigued, I ceased all effort and became motionless, suspended in a dark, watery limbo, wondering what to do next. *You know, if we were to open our eyes, that would help,* one side of my mind suggested. *Not a chance,* said the other.

Spit above the surface once again, I gasped in air and looked around, but my fear reinvigorated at the recognition that the raft was nowhere in sight.

From deep in my memory banks came an old camp counselor's voice: *Never panic. The water is far stronger than you are.* The phrase *never panic* reverberated in my head as I nearly redlined in fear. *Never panic ... never panic ... never panic...*

Never once had I ever cried out for help. Never once had I lost control. Never once had I felt so helpless. I would not allow myself to be the kind of person who was unable to fend for himself . . . but my primal fight-or-flight response pushed back, determined to be acknowledged. The peril I was in was no longer manufactured by my mind. I was in real, immediate danger.

A hot wave of sheer panic shot up from my toes and rose up through my body like a fireball.

"HELP!" I cried out, with every cell in my body shrieking along with me.

My shouting resulted only in a barely-audible whisper. Aghast, I called out a second time, to no avail. My petrified voice box had betrayed me. Voiceless, powerless, helpless, and completely on my own, my panic morphed into absolute horror.

My only chance of surviving was to reach that nearby rock. Summoning whatever strength I had left, I swam towards it with focused determination. *Three more arm lengths to go. Keep going. Two more arm lengths and I'll be safe.*

Extending my left arm for my next stroke, the forces of the river grabbed me by the waist and pulled me under again. Any remaining hope I had sank into the dark water along with my body. My muscles were out of fuel, my emotional wiring was fried, and my mind was devoid of any more ideas. A somber thought emerged: *I don't think I can do this.*

With nothing left to give, I surrendered into complete stillness, engulfed below the rapids in the soundless depths. The river held me, weightless. Time dissolved into nothingness.

In the darkness, faint, golden, geometric shapes started to form in my vision. The novelty of these images stirring to life behind my eyelids prompted a genuine curiosity, drawing my focus away from danger and into a sense of calm.

My inquiry into this mystical, time-suspended world was abruptly interrupted as my head was birthed through the surface of the water. In quick succession, I felt surprise, relief, and confusion as I found my bearings and I realized that I was somewhere new. No longer cycling around the eddy, I had been smoothly carried to the main body of the river and was being fluidly ushered downstream.

Like a mirage that became real, suddenly, there it was ... the designated purple rescue kayak. I grabbed onto the rope handle and was towed to the nearest raft.

"Climb on board!" I was instructed.

Part Two

Knowing that was an impossible task given my utter physical exhaustion, I managed to stammer, "I can't!"

I was grateful to have regained my voice, and that assistance had arrived after I had surrendered. This watery world helped me understand the power of letting go and trusting the greater forces at play, showing me that beyond my stifling comfort zone exists a soft, cushioned pathway to safety.

Two burly arms reached down to grab hold of my life preserver and pulled me into the belly of the raft. I laid there in total submission, flopping with the uncontrollable and unpredictable motion of the currents, until I was brought safely and gently to shore.

Dave Eyerman

MY FRIED THE FIRE

Whenever I'm around a fire, gazing into its dancing orange flames, all is right with the world. It is my escape, my friend, my protector. Whenever I'm nervous, anxious, or upset, this element helps me to relax and feel comforted. Sometimes, when I'm near a fireplace, I sit directly on the hearth, practically inside the firebox. Like having a heating pad on my back, its warmth soothes my body and nourishes my soul.

It was my father who built the fireplace in our family home and taught me how to responsibly start and tend a fire. I learned from him to respect fire, not fear it. It was always a small thrill to reach inside for the flue and hear the squeak of the damper being pushed open. The fresh scent of kindling laid on top of crumpled newspaper was the sweetest aroma ever.

Fire has taught me, too. In my early years of fire tending for the Native American sweat lodge ceremonies at the farm, the fires were always magical. I would gladly lug armloads of logs and rocks in preparation for them, and enjoyed the sense of accomplishment. At moments of rest during the ceremonies, I'd stare hypnotically into the flickering ribbons of light as they popped and crackled. When the head-sized rocks were red hot, they were ready to be pulled out of the fire with a pitchfork and brought into the lodge.

One evening, as the blazing fire began to settle and burn down, I noticed a rock exposed to the air, and knew that it needed to be covered to stay hot. I grabbed a log and moved fast towards the fire to cover the rock. A sudden gust of wind blew the fire directly at my face. I stepped back quickly with smoke stinging my eyes, and luckily did not get burned.

A few seconds later, I hastily went towards the fire again. As I leaned in, with a hissing sound, a wave of intense heat swept over me, and I felt a hot singe on my face.

Immediately, I pulled away from the heat and, with my hands, instinctively began using an energy healing technique that I'd learned years earlier. Within minutes, the pain on my seared face had subsided.

My friend, Sheri, sat down next to me as I combed the white ash out of my hair. It felt bristly and I got a whiff of what smelled like burning rubber.

"Did I just burn my hair?" I asked Sheri.

Her eyes widened as she examined my head. "Oh wow! Yes!"

Sheri made a dash for a pair of scissors in the prayer tie box, and gave me a haircut right then and there.

Since that experience, I've developed an even greater respect for and stronger relationship with Fire. I listen intently to it as I offer it sacred herbs of tobacco, flat cedar, sweet grass, and sage. In return, Fire gifts me with visions in its flames, such as faces melded from the rocks and wood, and objects so real that they look like photos placed inside its glowing embers. How these visions arise is a mystery for which I have no logical explanation. Maybe someday, I will.

One night, I had a beautiful and profound vision while sitting alone by the fire at the Lakota Sundance, an annual sacred ceremony of hard work and prayer that lasts eight days. Earlier that day, I had been gifted a piece of pipestone by a healer friend who had a dream that told her the stone was meant for me.

The ceremonial dance was over and my fire-keeping duties were done, and I was happy to sit and commune with the fire. In complete stillness, while contemplating my friend's extraordinary gesture, I dropped into a deep meditative state. With open eyes, the entire fire before me transformed into a woman holding a pipe, and the inspiration arose to craft a pipe from my gifted stone. In those moments, I can honestly say that I felt love for this powerful element, like one might have for a beloved family member.

"Talk to the fire," one of the medicine men used to tell me. "It's a relative."

It finally all made sense to me. In fact, I've come to understand that Fire loves me, too. I humbly come to it with personal questions and situations, and it offers guidance and healing for everything from intense headaches that I'd often get to answers about my life's direction.

Perhaps my most profound experience with Fire occurred at a council fire, where Sundance participants gather and share stories about their experiences during the dance. The fire consists of a ring of 50 rocks that are joined closely together like a jagged, 3D puzzle on the ground. On the last day of the dance, exhausted from tending fire the entire week, I plopped down on the wooden bench next to my friend, Ed. My ankles were swollen from standing for hours, and my fingers looked like sausages from stoking the fire, yet I was filled to the brim with joy and high-vibrational energy.

Satisfying my obsessive desire to feed the fire, I stood up, adjusted my long skirt, grabbed a piece of wood in my right hand, and knelt down, bracing myself with my other hand on the rock to my left. As I leaned in to place the wood in the fire, the rock gave way under my left hand, sending me tumbling head first straight into the fire.

Ed gasped as he scrambled to pull me from the center of the pit.

"Oh my gosh . . . are you alright, Sharon?"

"I'm fine." I shook my head in disbelief. "I think I'm fine."

"Are you sure? You were literally *in* the fire!"

"Yes, I'm sure."

Covered with ash and debris, Ed stared at me in astonishment that I had not sustained a single burn mark, and that my hair and clothing had not become engulfed in the flames. I knew beyond a doubt that Fire had protected me, like a cherished loved one. Still somewhat in awe after that experience, I remained in a state of grace and gratitude for the rest of the day.

Sharon M. Sirkis

MY CRYSTAL TEACHERS

I'm not sure what I was expecting—the worst, I think, but when you pray to God or ask the universe for what you want, you are given what you need. For some time, I had been training with a well-known psychic medium and healer, and one day, instead of learning untold secrets from Rose, my best teacher turned out to be a common quartz crystal.

While showing me how to sense energy currents for healing, Rose presented me with three small, single-terminated, clear quartz crystals that she had recently bought. She instructed me to close my eyes, put the crystals up to my third-eye chakra, one by one, get a sense of the crystal, and tell her who the crystal should be assigned to: me, my sister, Lisa, or my niece, Angela.

Rose often used competition as a motivational tool for testing and expanding our psychic abilities. It was just her teaching style and, in any case, it always made me anxious to want to do well with whatever exercise she gave me. I rushed into this exercise with no grounding, no focus, and not feeling very calm.

The first crystal that I picked up felt petite in my hand. One of its sides flashed a rainbow as the sun's rays touched it. It was beautiful and it warmed my heart. When I put the crystal to my brow, a smile came to my lips. The crystal felt upbeat and colorful, sociable, and happy.

I declared that my niece should work with this crystal. Angela, in her late teens at the time, had a sweet, charming way about her, and a large circle of friends with whom she went to lots of parties and events. This crystal seemed perfect for her. Rose smiled. Whew! That was easy. I guess there is more to stones than I knew.

The second crystal I picked up was the largest of the three. In my hand, this one felt more powerful and serious than the first. It was pristine, clear, and on the ready, as if it had a mission. I put it to my brow and felt an energy present that seemed normal and familiar. I pushed harder but got no further information for my effort. I put the crystal down and picked up the third one, with Rose watching intently the entire time.

Pressing on with even more determination, I couldn't read the energy of the third crystal. It was pretty to look at and maybe I was trying too hard, so I closed my eyes and touched it to my head.

As I did, my brow and the inside of my head lit up with a brilliant flash of red light. I heard an internal roar, coupled with the sound of cracking glass. Both my hand and the crystal involuntarily propelled themselves about 12 inches in front of me. It was as if the crystal was repulsed away from my head.

Stunned and a little dizzy, I paused for a few seconds to gather my composure. Looking at it with my physical eyes, what had appeared as a clear crystal just seconds before was now totally cloudy.

Many questions, feelings, and thoughts overpowered me at once. *What was that?* I sensed injury. *Was it my injury? My pituitary or pineal gland? My chakra center? Was the crystal injured?*

My head began to ache. *Was the crystal in pain? How can this be possible? What did I do? What should I do?*

All I could do was stand there, my hand shaking, my head throbbing, and afraid that I would be revisiting my lunch soon. As my eyes welled with tears, I felt horrified and saddened by whatever it was that had happened to this crystal. All I could do was stare at it and wonder what the story was behind all of this power and emotion.

Clearly seeing that I was in distress, Rose spoke something to me with concern in her voice and asked me to hand her the crystal. She immediately went to work sending healing energy to it. As if to console me, she mentioned something about giving the crystal to Lisa as an exercise in the healing work that she was learning at that time.

Come on, Lynne, it's just a stone, I rationalized, but no, it was more than that. Something visceral and very real had happened when I felt the red blast in my head and my hand being pulled away from it.

I often think of that crystal and feel deep gratitude for what it taught me. Crystals are living beings, and I should have asked its spirit for permission to read its energy. I know better now, and am more respectful and humble when approaching other sentient beings. Every one of them is a potential teacher.

Lynne D. Chown

LIFT OFF

As I left my home on the island of Kauai to return to Ohio, I was also leaving behind a career that I loved—a life in the sky, immersed in beauty beyond description, and a flying job that rewarded me with financial abundance.

My father was dying. I'd been the prodigal son for 25 years, but Dad needed me to return home for an indefinite amount of time to care for him as he prepared for his final journey.

While in Hawaii flying helicopter tours, I showed tourists the island's stunning beauty. Shaped like an artist's palette, Kauai drips with color. The lush jungle glistens after sudden tropic squalls. Riotous reds and pinks of ginger plants crowd every berm. Perfumed plumeria air their pungent aroma. One of my most favorite things about living in Kauai, though, was seeing rainbows almost every day.

I departed this Eden and was soon back in Columbus. At baggage claim, my sister gave me an update on the therapy that my siblings had elected for Dad based on his condition.

"How is he, sis?"

"He's in good spirits, but he doesn't have a lot of strength left." She sighed in frustration. "When we're about to give up, he rallies again."

"What about the therapies?"

"He calls them hocus pocus."

On the drive to our father's house, she described a confusing array of drugs, doctors' appointments, interruptions in Dad's routine, and a lack of the serenity he should be allowed to have at age 82. Listening to all of this, I sensed that Dad was hanging on just for us. He'd made important decisions all his life. Now his world was circumscribed, as if he were a child, and my siblings were asking him to defer to their judgment.

As I entered the house, my first view of my father filled me with pain. Dad struggled to stand then hobbled over to greet me.

"Hello, son," he said in a whisper.

Dropping my bag to embrace him, it shocked me how frail he'd become.

"Hi, Pop."

We hugged for a few long seconds. I felt his ribs, baggy shirt, and the frail arc of his shoulders. Bent at the waist, he shuffled back to his chair. Every labored step he took broke my heart. Just a few years before, he'd built a sturdy cabin with his own hands.

It had been years since I'd spent time with my father. He'd always been reluctant to talk about his life growing up on a farm. Entering the Navy in 1943, he served on a minesweeper. Post-war, he married my mother and worked as a carpenter, toiling to feed 10 kids.

Despite his admirable life, Dad seemed ashamed of his lack of worldly accomplishments, always deferring to those of his children; but he opened up to me, his second born and namesake, as we finally had a chance to catch up. It soon became apparent that if my trip from Hawaii to Ohio had been difficult for me, his journey from independent adult to a dependent elder had been harder.

The next day, I took Dad to his cancer specialist.

"I'll drive," I said, helping him into his little Chevy. "You can navigate."

"Fine," he agreed, sighing in resignation. "They told me not to drive anyway."

One afternoon while we talked in the living room, Dad asked, "Do you remember the fellow who rented our garage for 10 dollars a month?"

That was important extra cash for us in 1958, and that college student wanted a place to store his new Thunderbird, a gift from his doctor father.

"Remember him pulling the overhead door down after that heavy rain?" Dad smiled at the memory of the pool of water atop the door that gushed down.

"Took a soaking, didn't he?" Dad laughed. "He still paid his rent, though."

"Mom probably sent the money to some doctor who was soaking *us*," I added.

Dad looked away. "Probably so."

Mentioning our precarious financial status years ago, I again sensed his embarrassment. Despite his exhaustive efforts to care for us, money was always a sore spot. We'd never even ridden in a Thunderbird, let alone owned one.

"You must have been discouraged at times, huh Dad?" I said upon asking about his work-filled life.

"There were a few times," he agreed. "Like when Theresa was born, with all of her hospital bills, and when I wrecked the Pontiac, our only car."

"Would you do it all again?" I had to ask him.

With more vigor than he'd shown since my arrival, he nodded. "I wouldn't change a thing."

Behind the resignation in his eyes, I sensed that there was something he couldn't bring himself to say. Changing topics, he spoke of his youth and the war years.

Listening intently, I recalled an incident when I was 10 years old. He'd come home covered in grime and the pungent smell of another day of

Part Two

heavy, dusty work. His mouth slack with exhaustion, Dad scaled the steps of our back porch and plodded inside the house. Sweat stained his shirt, and sawdust flecked his arms.

My mother greeted him with news that the toilet was clogged again. Dad's knees nearly buckled, as another task demanded his attention. As he returned to the truck for his toolbox, in that instant, I knew what I didn't want: to be like my father with his hard, thankless life.

It seemed as if, by taking everything he could give and more, I'd caused him to lose his dreams . . . and his hard work allowed me to pursue mine.

"I was so proud of you," he said, unbidden. "Flying all that time, and doing it so well."

With those words, it was obvious that he'd known what I didn't want, and knew that I'd gotten what I did. I'd gone to Army flight school, been in a war, and had become highly decorated. Afterwards, I launched a flying career that spanned 35 years, traveling the world, doing what I loved. Not once had I come home covered in sawdust.

I heard something else in my father's reverie that afternoon. I heard gratitude, not at my return, but for listening to him, and really hearing what he wanted. The words broke my heart, but they were true, and perhaps they were the most important words we'd ever shared.

"They tell me I need to keep doing this," he said. "The chemo, and the hospital, and all the hocus-pocus."

"Who does?" I asked.

"Everyone. They tell me I should keep going. They mention new drugs and new therapies. They complain about how much weight I've lost, and say the doctor needs to give me a feeding tube." His eyes pooled with angry tears. "I don't want a damned feeding tube!"

The phone rang. It was my sister asking about Dad's pending visit to the cancer specialist. I put it on speakerphone, and her voice filled the room:

Who can take Dad to the doctor? Are you getting enough to eat? Is Dad keeping his medicine down?

The chorus of interventions and questions made my head swim. I'd heard what Dad had gone through for months, and how his wishes seemed to be drowned out in the cacophony. The vision of him coming home that night to a clogged toilet reappeared. In that moment, I understood that my trip to care for him was more than comfort . . . it was permission. I'd come to give him something that *he* wanted for a change.

"You look tired, Dad."

"Yes, I am."

He wanted to let go, quit the heroics, and be allowed to die. I heard something besides complaining, which he never did. My arrival was his chance to escape a life he'd been burdened with for too long. I held the power to help him take the final trip his way by giving him liftoff clearance from the cockpit.

For the first time in my life, I asked my father what I could do for him.

"Dad, what do you want?"

His eyes met mine. "Make them stop. Just make them stop."

Feeling our roles change, parent passing to son, the light of understanding warmed the room. I promised him I'd see to it. Against the wishes of my siblings and others, I ordered that Dad's treatments be stopped. They ended, and we waited.

That summer in Ohio, redbuds, violets, and assorted mid-western greenery was in bloom, but in the four months I'd been back, I saw no rainbows, and I missed them. In quiet moments, I pondered the physics of this weather phenomena, how they result from the separation of light into various wavelengths. I'd learned that as sunlight enters a raindrop, it bends. The light then contacts the opposite surface of each drop, reflects it back as if from a mirror, then glimmers out the other side, separating into the colors we see.

Part Two

I don't pretend to understand the arcane formulas of rainbow creation, and while playing among rainbows as I flew in Hawaii, I didn't include this information in my tour narrative. Like me, it seemed, tourists only wanted to see the ephemeral nature of things.

Similar to the support that wind provides while in flight, or my father's steady presence, I took rainbows for granted, not bothering to stop and consider their freely-given enrichment in my life.

The afternoon of September 30, as I prepared to go to Dad's house, my sister called. When I answered the phone, she was sobbing.

"Dad's gone. I was holding his hand ... and he just slipped away."

My father died in his own bed, in his own home, in his own way, unburdened. His was a good death, made more so, I'd like to believe, by my presence, the prodigal son back on solid ground after many years in the sky.

Around seven o'clock in the morning, the day after my father died, I readied for a full day of meeting friends and family, making funeral arrangements, and consoling each other. From the corner of my eye, I caught sight of the cresting sun as it streamed through my bedroom window.

As I pushed open the curtain, spilling light into the room, there it was: a double rainbow draped across the horizon, its rich tendrils of color dripping like watercolors from an artist's palette.

"Goodbye, Dad, and thank you for everything," I said. "You finally get your chance to fly."

Byron Edgington

SUNSHINE AND PAPA TREE

My heart sank as I called the veterinarian. My soulmate kitty, Sunshine, had a long history of dental infections, but when the vet confirmed my biggest fear, that he had mandibular cancer, it shook me to the core.

As an animal communicator, I would tell Sunshine to let me know when he was ready to go home and see his friend, Bo. Sunshine and Bo were great kitty friends until Bo crossed the Rainbow Bridge.

One day, I awoke to see Sunshine lying on his usual spot on the bed. I was guided to kneel at the foot of the bed, look my Sunshine boy in the eyes, and connect with him. I put my right-hand palm down in front of him and explained that when it was time, he needed to place his paw on my hand. I showed him how to do this by placing my left hand over my right hand. In astonishment, he did exactly that.

The next day was a major holiday and the veterinary offices were closed. That was one of the longest days of my life. Sunshine spent a lot of time on the patio, across from a beautiful nearby tree that I had named Papa. I sat outside with Sunshine, gently petting him and sharing all of the love I had for this dear boy.

When it was finally time, I numbly went through the motions at the vet's office, my heart breaking the entire time. After the long ordeal, I brought Sunshine home so that I could have a sacred service for him.

In the weeks and months to come, as I endured this loss and to heal my grief, I felt motivated to go outside, hug Papa, and talk to him regularly. This beautiful tree was like the loving grandfather I never had. Without a doubt, I knew that Papa understood everything I said and felt, including my tremendous love for Sunshine.

Time passed, and I learned that Papa, my beautiful tree, was dying and needed to be cut down. I explained all of this to Papa through tears. Papa responded that his consciousness would always be around, and that he would never be truly gone. I took some of Papa's bark and placed it on a beautiful container, like I often do with crystals.

Since then, there have been a number of times when I've sensed Papa's consciousness. Yet one of the most amazing experiences I had was quite recently, while sitting on the grass and leaning against another beautiful tree near my yard. This tree was located one patio over from where Papa used to proudly stand. As I connected to this particular tree and shared the story of Papa, I asked if he and Papa had ever communicated. Suddenly, I was bathed in the most profound feeling of unconditional Love that penetrated my entire being.

Who's love was it? The love of the cosmos? Papa? Sunshine? My new tree friend? In truth, it doesn't matter because we are all connected. We are all one. Love is always there and permeates all sentient beings if we allow ourselves to connect to it.

Victoria Ann Glod

THE MEDICINE WHEEL

*V*enturing into the alpine forest on a crisp autumn day, my intention was to find the perfect rock. Several of my mentors had been sharing with me about the profound process of rock sitting, and I was inspired to try connecting with the natural world in this new way.

As I walked the rustic trails and glanced around the woods, I searched for rocks large enough to comfortably sit on. I'd learned that due to the harmonic nature of rocks, merging with their essence would open me to the potential of directly receiving insights and information that I could tangibly utilize in my own life, especially in relation to my soul's work. For the rest of the day, I played with this technique by sitting on various stones and discerning the distinctions in their vibrations.

Upon returning home from my nature walk, I was eager to incorporate this practice into my daily routine. I spent the next few weeks seeking out sizeable rocks around my local area, inquiring about their interest in collaborating with me, and getting to know each of them. Several spoke to me through their energetic resonance and they became my "go to" rocks.

As I formed a relationship with these stone beings, I learned a lot about the nature of rocks and their energetic abilities to transmit frequencies. They taught me how humans can collaborate with them, and how doing so helps us on our path of expansion and unity consciousness. After these delightfully peaceful stone sessions, as I call them, I always parted their company feeling better, lighter, more hopeful, and even inspired.

One morning, after hanging out with my favorite rocks, I began to walk the nearby land in meditation. Coming across a clearing in the trees, I stopped in my tracks. Curiously, I had walked this portion of the landscape innumerable times, but this time, it felt different. Something, or someone, was compelling me to pay attention and listen for an important reason.

As I connected through my intuition to this circular space in the clearing, a stunning and detailed vision formed in my mind's eye. Plain as day, I saw the stone formation of an ancient medicine wheel about 15 feet in diameter, with four large rocks, one or two feet in diameter, delineating each of the four directions. Smaller stones filled in the spaces between the large rocks to complete the circle. A straight line of stones connected each of the directional rocks to the center of the circle. In the center was another gathering of stones, creating a small fire ring.

Of course! I thought. *This land wants to be a medicine wheel.*

My heart expanded at the idea and I was overcome with gratitude for this amazing revelation. In awe of this inner vision, I immediately had a deep knowing that this revealing was directly connected to my recent time spent sitting on and connecting to the rocks. Feeling intensely moved that something profound was about to be shown to me, I couldn't wait to begin the work of gathering the rocks and stones that would like to participate in this hallowed project.

Years earlier, I had been initiated in the tradition of working with a medicine wheel. It's a sacred and personal practice that I've carried with me in various forms, usually on a small scale of simply working with stones representing the four directions and four elements. Somehow, I knew that I would someday create a larger, more permanent medicine wheel to incorporate into my shamanic practice. That time had now come.

With permission granted by the land, my beloved partner and I began gathering stones and rocks that were willing to be a part of this sacred circle. Both of us felt the reverence of this process as specific stones stepped forward to work with us. In keeping with our intention to honor nature, we were conscious to disturb as little of the earth as possible. Instead of digging holes, we laid each stone on top of the ground. Living in the Rocky Mountains made it easy to find stones above ground.

My mind's vision began to come to life as we prepared to place the four large directional stones and then fill in the perimeter with smaller ones. As we set the larger stones, we observed something quite interesting on the ground. Four directional stones, each about two feet in diameter, appeared to already be in place. Each was embedded in the ground, as if they had been in these positions for a long time. Curious, we searched in the immediate area yet found no other rocks of this size. The more we looked at the position of the four stones, the clearer it became that they were placed there intentionally.

"Wow! It looks like we are not the first ones to feel compelled to create a medicine wheel in this space," I said to my beloved, and he felt this, as well.

Adding to the peculiarity of this discovery was the history of this area. We knew that before we had moved there, cattle grazed in the area, but there had been no human settlement. We checked these preexisting stones with the compass and discovered that each one matched within a few degrees of each direction. We were in absolute awe, as we knew that this was no accident; the odds of this randomly happening were extremely rare.

The higher message was now clear: This wasn't a space that *wanted* to be a medicine wheel; rather, it had *already been* a medicine wheel! The true sacredness of the site was coming to light before our very eyes. We felt both humbled and emotionally overwhelmed to be the ones helping the guardians of this land. Now understanding the energetic imprinting that was already present in the existing directional stones, we could consciously choose to honor and work with them by recreating the wheel, with these newly revealed ancient stones as the wisdom keepers.

Over the years, this medicine wheel has become an integral part of my spiritual practice and has served as a major conduit for strengthening my relationship with the natural world. Walking the wheel, praying, meditating, and offering ceremony has helped me to more fully receive and understand the messages coming from the Divine. The guidance, support, and wisdom that permeates through nature provides me with a higher understanding of myself and my relationship with all of creation.

In fact, before I penned these words, I was called to do a ceremony at the medicine wheel, asking its blessing to share this story. With my medicine bag holding my offerings of sage and cedar, I headed out to the land with my best pal, Astro, a Great Dane. He has been walking the wheel with me for years and it's always fascinating to watch his behavior change from sniffing everything to standing at attentive presence by my side at the wheel. He's a wonderful ally to help ground and amplify the intentions and energy.

As the sacred stone circle came into view, I felt some nervousness around my request to share the medicine wheel story, as this had been, up until this point, an intimate personal practice and experience for me alone. I greeted the wheel reverently and approached the directional stone of the east, pertaining to new possibilities and opportunities. Knowing that this direction also correlates with the element of air, I asked it to source me in transcending my thinking mind and connecting to Divine intelligence.

Placing one hand on my heart and the other on Astro's back, I brought my attention to my breath. Taking a deep inhale through my nose and pausing before exhaling, slowly and completely, I used sound to help move the energy that was building up in my body. I repeated this rhythmic breathing cycle multiple times until I felt deeply grounded, calm, and present.

Then I reached into my medicine bag, taking a pinch each of the sage and cedar. Holding them to my heart, I said a prayer of gratitude for all the ways nature sources and sustains my life, and placed the offering on top of the east stone.

As I spoke the opening invocation out loud, two deer meandered into a nearby clearing to the north, the direction of the element of earth and the ancestors. Astro watched them but didn't move. The deer reminded me of the gentle allure to new adventures such as this one, as well as the power of returning to traditional ways. I took this as a positive sign.

We continued to move around the wheel, finishing in the center by placing a final offering there. Sitting in meditation at the completion of the ceremony, I couldn't help but notice a Clarke nutcracker squawking loudly as it flew in from the north side of the wheel to the south, which represents the element of fire and being in one's full expression. This species of bird showing up to participate in the ceremony seemed especially auspiciousness, as these nutcrackers are known to carefully hide a few seeds at a time in various places in order to be found later for nourishment.

The parallel of my rediscovering the ancient medicine wheel was not lost on me. It was set in place, perhaps millennia ago, by the ancestors ... only to be revealed in this 21st century. It is still serving its sacred role of nourishing our human remembrance of the power of nature.

Ana Maria Vasquez

PART THREE

Deepening Your Connection with Nature

The clearest way into the Universe is through a forest wilderness.

—JOHN MUIR

PRACTICES TO DEEPEN YOUR NATURE EXPERIENCES

*T*he entry point for attuning more fully to the mystical forces of nature is paying attention to its nuances. Even if you traverse the same walking trail in your neighborhood on a regular basis or breeze by the same row of shrubs, rocky cliffs, meandering creek, or rural farms every day, nature is always willing to offer surprising and delightful new experiences. Depending on the time of day or season, its cycles are never static. Like a reliable best friend, you can always count on nature to provide caring support, guidance, and wisdom.

The more you connect with the natural realm and honor its bountiful gifts, the more it reveals to you. This is not some sort of mystical teaching, but rather a universal truth. The trees, plants, stones, and landscapes can become your powerful allies and unlimited sources of joy, energy, and inspiration.

As with other spiritual practices like meditation, prayer, chanting, yoga, and shamanic journeying, cultivating an ongoing devotion to nature will enable you to slow down and reflect on situations in your everyday life before responding to them. The following simple techniques can serve to move you into a state of presence, raising your vibration with grace and ease, so that you can receive clearer and more concise messages from Nature.

Part Three

EARTHING

Our ancestors instinctually knew that walking barefoot and sleeping on the ground enabled them to sync with the earth's healing energy. The earth produces a constant flow of free electrons with a negative charge, and we need these electrons for our well-being. Even for us modern humans, establishing a foundational connection to nature is as easy as grounding.

Also referred to as earthing, this is the simple process of coming into physical contact with Gaia by walking barefoot on grass, sand, dirt, or rock. When your bare feet or skin touch the earth, these electrons are pulled up into your physical and energetic body. Considered nature's most powerful antioxidants, these electrons neutralize the electromagnetic fields and free radicals we're bombarded with in our 21st century lifestyle, from our mobile phones and microwaves to cell towers and synthetic materials in our homes and clothing. These EMFs and free radicals damage our tissues and cells, contributing to inflammation, aging, and disease. Counteracting them through earthing allows the body to naturally repair and heal itself. This is another incredible gift that Mother Earth provides to us and all living beings on the planet. For that reason alone, she deserves our gratitude.

To practice grounding, stand barefoot or lie on the grass or somewhere that allows your body to be in direct contact with the ground. Get comfortable, take a few deep breaths, and clear your mind. Offer a few words—silent or spoken—of respect to the earth, which can be as simple as *thank you*. Allow yourself to drop into a heart space to activate heart coherence with Gaia.

Stay in this space of receptivity for as long as you'd like. Earthing can be effective even if done for as little as five minutes on a regular basis. This may not sound like a long time, but consider you have 50,000 to 80,000 receptors on the bottoms of your feet absorbing this generous provision of earth energy.

Earthing allows us to sync up with nature's high frequencies, making it easier to connect to and interpret messages from nature.

TREE HUGGING

If you've never hugged a tree, I highly recommend doing it . . . and often! This simple ritual of making physical contact with powerful tree beings can greatly awaken your senses, release feel-good hormones like oxytocin and dopamine, and guide you into a calm state of presence. It's a full physical and spiritual body experience.

We all know how good it feels to hug a loved one or cherished animal. Now imagine being infused with love from the actual source that produces life-giving oxygen for you. Here is your chance to thank one of your tree brothers for this essential element—the gift of breath.

To begin, choose a tree in your backyard or at a local park. Approach the tree, observing it carefully. Ask permission to hug the tree. Once you sense an affirmative response, take a few deep breaths, wrap your arms as far around the trunk as they'll go, then lean in. Place your cheek gently against the bark and observe the warmth and currents flowing from this amazing being and into you. Close your eyes and take a moment to feel the bark with your hands and arms.

Continue hugging the tree for a minimum of 21 seconds, which is the time it takes for the feel-good hormones to be released in your body and to calibrate to the tree's frequency. As you connect with the tree, notice how it makes you feel. How does it smell? What do you hear? Open your mouth and see if you taste anything in the air. Touch a leaf if one is within reach.

If you have an intention, hold it lightly in your mind, then release all thought and allow for messages from the tree to come through. Be sure to hold the space for any needs the tree may have as well. When this process feels complete, step back from the tree. Thank it for raising your vibration and filling you with not only its energy but also the energy of Mother Earth. Journal any thoughts, feelings, or sensations that came to you while engaged in this shared process.

When it's too cold to be outside or during inclement weather, a great alternative is to put your hands on a houseplant. As you connect with different trees and plants over time, notice the variations in their energy and the messages you receive from them.

The truth is that you don't even have to physically hug the tree—simply being in the tree's auric field or even visualizing yourself there will allow for the connection to take place and your vibration to be raised.

STONE SITTING AND GAZING

Another simple technique for connecting with nature that yields tremendous results is stone sitting and gazing. How many times have you walked past a rock without being conscious of its energetic presence? This is a casual yet compelling way to connect with these solidly powerful beings.

Commence by asking a rock, standing stone, or boulder—either out in nature or one in your living environment—to work with you. Be mindful of choosing a rock that has enough surface to sit upon. Ask permission and use your intuitive senses to confirm a positive response.

Sit on the rock and consciously connect your tailbone to its surface, initiating the flow of energy. Alternatively, you can place your bare feet on the surface of the stone. Sit or stand quietly and begin to get curious about what the stone might want to impart to you—either messages or inherent qualities such as stability or steadfastness. What do you see, hear, or smell? Where is your attention drawn? How do you feel about all of it? Thank the stone for its insights and journal about the experience.

To engage with these beings through gazing, choose a stone, boulder, or rock formation. Sit quietly with your eyes open and breathe steadily. Soften your gaze and focus your attention on the rock. In your mind, take note of anything you see on the face of the rock or around it, like hawks flying overhead or the sun cresting behind it. If you see any movement, shapes, or shadows, stay focused on the rock in front of you. Do this for as long as you feel comfortable, remaining open to any high vibrational communication.

When this feels complete, thank the rock for its alliance and journal about what you saw in your outer or inner vision. You can repeat the same exercise, asking a question beforehand, and then journal the answers you receive.

FOREST BATHING

When you do have more time to spend in nature beyond earthing, hugging a tree, or stone sitting, I recommend taking a leisurely walk in a wooded area and experimenting with the practice of forest bathing, a term coined in the 1990s by the Japanese Ministry of Agriculture, Forestry, and Fisheries.

While hiking is typically something you do with a destination in mind, forest bathing focuses on the journey itself. The aim of this meditative practice is to slow down and heighten your present-moment awareness enough to immerse yourself in the beauty of the natural environment to the fullest extent possible.

Once you've arrived at the locale for your forest bathing ritual, turn off your mobile phone, clear your mind, and begin walking in a contemplative fashion along the trail, river's edge, mountain pass, or wherever you are. Engage all of your senses as you observe everything in this untouched setting. Do you hear the singsong of birds leaping from branch to branch or the scurrying of squirrels up tree trunks? Run your fingers across tree bark or mossy stones. Take in the citrusy or floral scents emanating from nearby fruits and flowers. Feel the leaves crunching underfoot. Look with fresh eyes at the shapes of tree nuts, rocks, and the undulating ripples of the water in the stream. Listen closely to what each of these living beings has to tell and teach you.

Give each glorious detail your full presence. How do you feel? Watch for patterns and keep a journal tracking your experiences. Forest bathing at dawn or dusk adds even more potency to the experience, as these are the times when the physical and spiritual realms intersect most easily.

At the completion of your walk, notice how you feel versus when you first set out. Express your appreciation to the forest, and when you depart from your excursion, honor it with a simple bow or prayer of thanks.

SACRED HERBAL STONE BATH

A simple herbal stone bath can raise your vibration, refresh your body and spirit, and strengthen your connection with nature. Before you luxuriate in this cleansing ritual, set the intention to connect deeply with nature and be open to all the possible ways that nature may creatively speak to you.

Ponder your intention as you quietly gather various stones, crystals, leaves, herbs, flowers or flower essences, pinecones, essential oils, twigs, and other natural elements that you feel instinctually drawn to. Remember to ask permission from each of these natural elements, assessing their willingness to collaborate with you during this sacred bath.

While running your water at a comfortably warm temperature, gently place your assembled items in a swath of cheesecloth or a cotton bandana, forming a makeshift medicine pouch. With your intention at the forefront of your thoughts, drop the pouch into the running water while thanking these nature playmates for their support.

Step into the tub, placing a comfy pillow behind your head for support, if desired. As you soak in the scented healing water for at least 20 minutes, notice how the frequencies from those natural elements infuse into your auric field and physical body. Clear your mind of everything, including your intention, and remain in a mode of pure receptivity as the heat and steam rise from the water's surface. Notice any new sensations, feelings, or thoughts that bubble up. If you'd like, keep a notebook nearby so you can jot them down.

When you are complete, give thanks once more for the gift of water and the items in your medicine pouch. Wrap yourself in a warm, fleecy towel, and as you dry off, vow to release anything that isn't serving your highest good. As you empty the tub, consciously watch any worries or concerns swirl into the drain and down to the earth to be transmuted. Unravel your medicine pouch and place the items in a special place outside.

Rinse and repeat whenever you need a fresh boost from nature.

NATURAL HOT SPRINGS

The rejuvenating powers of natural hot springs have been well-substantiated for thousands of years—everything from stress reduction and muscle recovery to improved circulation and pain relief. While these healing qualities of geothermal springs and the health-boosting minerals they contain is wonderful, the experience can be taken to an even deeper level by making a conscious connection with these natural elements. Due to the harmonics of the rocks and minerals and the conductive properties of the element of water heated by the element of fire from deep within the earth, you will be bathed in high frequencies and negative ions to elevate your mind, body, and soul. I frequent natural hot springs when I embark on any new creative projects.

Similar to the sacred herbal stone bath ritual above, set an intention upon entering the hot springs, asking the minerals for their support and thanking them for the healing they are bringing forth on your behalf. You can also connect with the benevolent ancestors who frequented the sacred healing waters. They understand the human condition and have wisdom to offer.

As you soak, remain open to receiving messages from the minerals, rocks, ancestors, and elements of fire and water.

If you are fortunate enough to live near or travel to the many regions around the world where hot springs have naturally formed, take advantage of this gift from nature. Here are a few of the common minerals found in natural hot springs and the benefits that you will receive while immersed in this mystical mineral experience:

- **Sodium** plays a pivotal role in enzyme operations and nerve and muscle function. It's also a mineral that assists in the conduction of energy and the flow of intuitive messages.
- **Lithium** elevates the mood and produces a sense of calm, allowing us to relax into expansive possibilities.
- **Magnesium** increases energy levels and assists with brain balance. It is a natural muscle relaxant and supports the brain in receiving intuitive messages.
- **Iron** is vital for blood health and increases resistance to disease. It is reflected in the blood within our bodies and provides a resonance with the natural world. This resonance creates an automatic flow of high vibrational information.

DOWSING

You may have heard of dowsing as a means of finding water underground, but from a spiritual perspective, it runs deeper than that. Dowsing is an ancient form of divination that can be used to interact with the energy of the natural world with tools called dowsing rods.

Throughout the book, I talk about asking permission to see if something in the natural world is willing to work with you. Dowsing is at the center of getting the answer. The body sway method of leaning forward for a yes and backwards for a no is a form of dowsing using the body as a dowsing rod.

While no one knows for sure how dowsing works, the consensus is that it has to do with energetics and your inherent ability to sense subtle shifts in the energy field around you. The sensing of the shift in the energy field is then demonstrated through the tool being used, which can be rods, pendulums, or the body.

Here's a fun and insightful experience you can have by dowsing the aura of a tree. Find a tree that is willing to do this experiment with you. Once you have a tree partner, stand with your back to the tree's trunk and say, "Tree, show me your aura." Walk slowly away from the tree, holding out your dowsing rod in front of you.

At some point, you will notice that suddenly the dowsing rod will move. When that happens, it's indicating the outside edge of the tree's aura. Mark this spot on the ground as a reference point. When you look up, you'll notice that you'll most likely be right under the dripline of the tree. The dripline is a good indicator for the average auric field of a tree.

Walk back up to the tree and thank it, showing it love. Tell this tree how magnificent it is, then once again, stand with your back to the tree's trunk and say, "Tree, show me your aura." Walk slowly away from the tree, holding out your dowsing rod. You will notice that it's at least four, five, or six feet further out than it was the first time. This time when you look up, you'll see there's no tree there, but the energy has expanded. The aura expands when you acknowledge a tree, give it love, and communicate with the tree.

MEDICINE WHEEL

Throughout history, our ancestors gathered around stone circles, believing them to be sacred spaces. The stones, directions, and elements have been

Three

for us to remember our alliance. The Medicine Wheel teaches us about balance. As we work with the wheel to heal ourselves, we are also healing Mother Earth. Before you begin working with the Medicine Wheel, an understanding of the four directions and four elements is integral to your process.

THE FOUR DIRECTIONS

- **East:** dawn, possibility, spring, illumination, birth, healing for the mind. Call on the direction of the east when you're starting a new project or need inspiration or mental clarity.
- **South:** noon, growth, summer, trust, adolescence, healing for the emotions. Call on the direction of the south when you need support around being in your full expression.
- **West:** dusk, integration, autumn, intuition, adulthood, healing for the spirit. Call on the direction of the west when you need to integrate everything you've been learning or need to merge with your higher self.
- **North:** midnight, vision, winter, wisdom, elder, ancestors, healing for the body. Call on the direction of the north when you want to be in deep listening and would like to invite in the wisdom of your ancestors.

THE FOUR ELEMENTS

- **Air:** life force energy, inspiration, mind, knowledge. Air helps us get out of our heads and connect to Divine intelligence.
- **Fire:** transformation, masculine energy, action, creativity, passion, light. Fire helps us ignite our passion and burns away the old, leaving only what is authentic.
- **Water:** surrender, flow, feminine energy, change, emotions. Water aids us in navigating the ebb and flow of life.

- **Earth:** grounding, manifestation, abundance, fertility. Earth helps us ground deeply and listen, connecting us with all that is.

The Medicine Wheel is a physical representation of the energies of the four directions and the four elements and our spiritual connection to each part. That's only the beginning, as various aspects of the wheel correlate with animals, plants, minerals, colors, time of day, stages of life, the moon, and the calendar. As you work with the Medicine Wheel, you embark on a journey that explores your interconnectedness with all of life force energy. This is a sacred and ancient tool that assists with the ebb and flow of life, helping you connect, grow, and transform. The wheel gives you a holistic view of the world and all of life. The more you connect with the Medicine Wheel, the more that is revealed to you about yourself and the wheel.

The easiest way to begin working with the Medicine Wheel is to find four stones willing to work with you to serve as wisdom keepers by delineating the four directions. You can do this on a small scale in your home on a table or at your desk. Additionally, you can build a larger wheel that allows you to physically walk the wheel. Whether it's four small pebbles on a section of your desk or a large wheel that you can physically walk outdoors, creating ongoing collaborations with the wheel are best regarded as ceremony, with reverence, respect, and an open heart and mind.

As you deepen your personal practice with the Medicine Wheel, you may be called to expand on it by adding a center stone to your four directional stones or adding stones to the circumference of the circle or to the quadrant lines going from the directional stone to the center. A complete traditional medicine wheel will typically contain 36 stones, building on those four directional stones and adding aspects of the moon, animals, plants, minerals, ancestors, and other ways that we are interconnected to the world around us. Collaborating with the Medicine Wheel is a dynamic and ever-evolving personal practice.

rough ceremony with the wheel, you begin with the request to deepen connection and awareness of the natural world and the life force energies that source and create her. As your awareness and connection cultivates, you can bring your questions, concerns, and intentions to your time with the wheel. The vortex that is created by intentionally and prayerfully placing the stones and calling on them to serve as wisdom keepers creates a powerful amplification of the energy, which you can consciously work with to amplify your intentions and help release that which no longer serves you in your life.

To begin ceremony with the Medicine Wheel, you can start with the *Invocation of the Natural Realm* below. Standing outside of the wheel, take three to four deep, slow, and complete breaths to help ground and become present. You can read the invocation out loud or silently to yourself.

INVOCATION OF THE NATURAL REALM

I come into union, alignment, and collaboration with all Life Force Energy.
I invoke and activate my sacred alliance with
the animals, the plants, the minerals, the elementals,
the four directions, the four elements,
the benevolent ancestors, the unseen high vibrational allies,
my Higher Self and the Divine.
I activate my field with Divine protection, insight, healing, wisdom, and guidance.
I'm in deep gratitude for the time and space to have these soulful connections.
And so it is.

When complete, you are now ready to walk the wheel. It is customary to walk the wheel in a clockwise fashion. If you are working with a large scale wheel, physically stand by the stone delineating the direction of the east and face the east. If you are working with a small scale wheel, you can simply stand near your four stones while facing the direction of the east. You can read the prayer for each direction out loud or silently to yourself.

Spirit of the East, I call on you.
Element of Air, help breathe me.
Eagle, Hawk, Owl, Raven, Woodpecker, and all wind flyers,
Please help me walk the Sacred Way.

Take a couple deep breaths and feel deeply into that prayer. When you're ready, turn to the right to face the direction of the south, or walk to the southern directional stone and face the south.

Spirit of the South, I call on you.
Element of Fire, fire flower, please blossom in my soul.
Cougar, Wolf, Coyote, Mouse, Snake,
Please help me walk the Sacred Way.

Take a couple deep breaths and feel deeply into that prayer. When you're ready, turn to the right to face the direction of the west, or walk to the western directional stone and face the west.

Spirit of the West, I call on you.
Element of Water, please help me move through my life
in rhythm with your ebb and flow.
Whale, Dolphin, Seal, Otter, please embrace me,
Please help me walk the Sacred Way.

Take a couple deep breaths and feel deeply into that prayer. When you're ready, turn to the right to face the direction of the north, or walk to the northern directional stone and face the north.

Spirit of the North, I call on you.
Element of Earth, help me ground and deeply listen.
Great Horned Ones, Buffalo, Moose, Elk, Deer, Antelope,
Please assist me.
Please help me walk the Sacred Way.

Take a couple deep breaths and feel deeply into that prayer. When you're ready, you can walk to the center of the circle. If you're working with a small-scale wheel, simply turn to face your wheel. Place your hands on your heart while reciting the end of the prayer.

Spirit Above, Father Sky, I feel you.
Your sunlight warms and lightens me.
Thank you for your Light.
Please help me walk the Sacred Way.

Spirit Below, Mother Earth, I come to you.
With all my heart I ask to receive your wisdom.
Please connect with me and help me
Walk the Sacred Way.

Spirit Within, I AM, I call on you.
Please merge me with my Higher Self's intention.
Deeply and interconnected let us travel.
Please remind me that I AM the Sacred Way.

And so it is.

At this point you can bring any of your personal questions, requests, or intentions. You can speak them out loud or acknowledge them silently. You are conversing with life force energy, so be sure to bring your authentic self and your integrity.

This is an ancient, sacred tool for connecting with the Divine through the natural world. Different cultures and traditions have their own ways of working with the wheel and even the symbology and locations of the various attributes of the wheel may differ. It's important to find a practice and layout that resonates for you.

BRING NATURE HOME

When you can't be out in nature, you can still connect to that flow of energy by bringing nature into your home. You may have actual aspects of nature placed around your home like pinecones, sticks, or rocks. You can fill your home with flowers, plants, and small trees, remembering to always begin by asking permission.

Include art that conveys the natural realm, like a painting of a meadow in bloom with wildflowers or a carving of a tree in a piece of driftwood. Watch videos and documentaries about nature. Set your screensavers, wallpapers, and backgrounds to your favorite nature images. Play plant music in the background or music that incorporates nature's sounds. You can work with herbs and oils through teas, using a diffuser for essential oils, and burning or smudging plant bundles. Ask the plants to help you with any intentions you have.

If you are purchasing these beings for your home, be sure to bring as much consciousness to the exchange as possible. If you can research to determine which supplier is bringing honor to the process, that would be best. You would want to know if their planting, growing, and harvesting practices are sustainable and care for the earth and its inhabitants. Those that utilize harmful chemicals do not honor the earth or the other beings, including humans who come into contact.

It's also important to remember that when we are unable to access the natural world, we are still infinite beings and have the ability to connect energetically, regardless of our location, indoors or outdoors. This is a great way to build and grow our intuitive muscles.

STUDY SACRED GEOMETRY

Sacred geometry is the blueprint, the building blocks, through mathematics for all of creation. It is the gateway to interconnectedness. Through mathematics, it describes the inner workings of nature and the intrinsic order of the universe. Those repeating patterns that we see in the natural world underscore the underlying geometry in nature. It is shapes in nature, fractals, recurring patterns, and ratios. Leonardo da Vinci illustrated both the mathematical proportions of the human body, which are based on ratios of 1.618, the sacred mean, and the concept of "squaring the circle" with his famous drawing *Vitruvian Man*.

The ancients understood and incorporated sacred geometry into their stone circles, pyramids, and temples. They had an understanding of how this geometry both harnessed and amplified the energy of the surrounding environment.

We can incorporate sacred geometry to increase our connection with the natural realm. For instance, if we look at the auric field of a tree from the perspective of looking down on it, we will see a circle, or a sphere, that would be the predominant shape of that tree's auric field. If there are two other trees in proximity and their canopies overlap, that means that their auric fields overlap as well. The space where those spheres of auric fields overlap creates the sacred geometry shape known as the *Vesica Pisces*, also known as a point of creation. We can work with trees in this configuration to help amplify our intentions for what we are manifesting in our lives. This potency also creates a magnification of whatever we want to release that may be getting in the way of our manifestations.

Even a seemingly simple stone circle can access the energy of the local environment, augmenting the effectiveness of our intentions by directing and focusing the flow of that energy in a way that supports our purpose of collaborating with the natural world. Each of the stones in that circle are emitting a frequency, and the shape of the circle creates a vortex within the circle. Look for the foundational sacred geometry shapes of spheres and triangles occurring organically in nature. As an infinite being, we can direct that energy through our intention as we work with energetics.

INTENTIONAL TEA TIME

We know that we are shifting from doing things *to* the plants, to collaborating *with* them. A beautiful place to incorporate that shift is with drinking tea, turning a simple act of drinking a cup of tea into a mystical ceremony.

When we are making a tea, we are working with the plant's essence mixed with the element of water. What a beautiful gathering of natural realm allies. The herb, oil, or plant that you use provides an herbal infusion of high vibrational frequencies and plant intelligence in addition to that flavor and aroma. Remember to invoke your alliance with the plant and ask for its assistance.

Bring all your physical and intuitive senses to the table for this tea party. Begin with gratitude to the plant and the water for sharing themselves in this way. Set any intentions you have for this tea ceremony. For example, you've been up against deadlines at work and you're not sure how you're going to get everything done on time. You may choose to work with the chamomile or lavender plant for its calming and soothing abilities. As you boil the water, be in a space of gratitude for this vital element and how it will work in synergy with the plant material to deliver the tea to you. Ask the water to help you be in the flow in your life in a greater way.

As you add the tea bag or plant material to the water, thank the plant for its essence, insights, and wisdom. Smell the aroma rising from the cup. Feel the warmth of the cup. Be open for the insights and guidance to come through. Through this time being in ceremony, you may begin to realize that it's not through tense, rigid, driven energy that you will meet your goal. Rather, aligning with nature's gentle rhythm will allow you to be in the flow and open to inspiration and Divine intervention.

Be in gratitude to your natural allies for everything that has come through during your time together. You may walk away from that tea ceremony with some immediate realizations of where to direct your energy and attention or even something that could help your productivity. Remember to say thank you.

When experimenting with any or all of the above practices, try to commune with nature in solitude. The mystical connections that nature is ready and willing to bring forth happen more easily when you're able to be in a natural setting without distraction. If you're hiking a trail or snowshoeing in the mountains with friends, kindly ask to have some time to venture alone, or at the very least, to walk in silence for part of the time. Better yet, invite them to participate in a few minutes of silence and then share your experiences.

WE ARE NATURE

*A*s human beings, we not only come from nature, we *are* nature. It's only since our ancestors moved out of the woods and other natural settings that we started to forget this part of our birthright. When we look at this long view of our human existence, there is really nothing for us to learn about connecting with nature; it's simply about remembering who we are.

When we remember our inherent connection with the life force energy that shows up in nature, we begin to subtly recalibrate to the refined frequencies that run through it. There is nothing more powerful than joining with this creative force that animates through not only us, but the trees, plants, soil, rocks, water, and air. With every breath we take, we involuntarily move this energy into our bodies and cells. It only makes sense to be aware of this and to collaborate with this life force.

As we open to this sentient world and align with the higher vibration of nature, we can begin to consciously rekindle and utilize these earth energies in our daily lives. This is where the magic really begins to happen. With reverence towards the process of attunement with nature, you reach a point where you are able to intentionally invoke these earth energies to help support you in moving through circumstances in your everyday life. It's a heart and mindset shift beyond just admiring the beauty of nature—which is astounding enough—into viewing it as an ally in your intuitive and spiritual development cycle.

You can begin by feeling the energy emanating from a landscape or sensing strength and protection from a stone when you most need those attributes. Perhaps you will stop in your tracks to experience the wind precisely when you need gentle encouragement, allowing the winds of change to blow through your life without fear. Or you may find yourself looking at a stunning photograph of an aspen grove, in their on-fire display of autumn colors, exactly when you need a role model for the beauty of impermanence and the hope of personal transformation.

It can be tremendously exciting to co-create with the greatest creator of all. And this magic shouldn't be a rare or obscure thing. Think of it this way: Partnering with nature is like having the most intelligent and intuitive GPS ever invented. You can go anywhere or ask to be driven anywhere with full assurance that your navigator understands everything about the best way to get you where you're destined to go—even if you don't yet know yourself.

I do believe that more of us are instinctually reestablishing this essential partnership with nature. I see in my work every day that more and more individuals are curious about the mystical qualities of nature and are interested in taking entire courses of study on rocks, trees, crystals, or plants. We're realizing that we've been missing that intimate connection with the earth, and all the comforts of modern-day society do not make up for that primal relationship in our lives. I'm also hearing from more and more people about mystical experiences they are having in nature, some of them in their own backyards. More individuals are reaching out to me for validation that a bush could possibly communicate with them. I reassure them that this is part of their spiritual expansion, a remembrance of our connection to all things.

Partnering with the natural world is the next level of our evolutionary development, while at the same time, a return to what our ancestors have known and done in the past. We know the power of the frequency created in prayer circles and meditation groups, when compassionate individuals hold the space for each other. Think of the incredibly positive outcomes that can be created for humanity if more of us collaborated with nature. In doing so, there's that equal exchange of energy amplifying those prayers and intentions. Many of us know the power of this in our human interactions, and how joining together for work projects, civic causes, rescue efforts, and to solve problems can positively affect outcomes. Now take it up to the level of being in communion with nature—perhaps our greatest teacher of presence, wonder, patience, freedom, simplicity, and intelligence—and imagine the power!

The practices that we are discussing here about how to enter two-way conversation with trees, plants, stones, and landscapes are geared towards experiencing the fullness of what we're naturally wired to do. As we step into co-creating with nature, we're no longer just asking for what we need or what nature can do for us as either an energetic being or as a physical resource. The dialogue becomes one of how we can source each other. We move into true collaboration with the trees, plants, stones, and landscapes so we can all receive an equal exchange of energy. It becomes a true relationship.

History has shown that we've been able to make big things happen and get things done while not being consciously connected to our surrounding land and its abundance. What I've learned is that this one-dimensional approach of forging ahead, separate from nature, is now an old way of doing things. Asking the land, the rocks, the soil, the native plants, and other natural elements in a geographic space what they want to be, in relation with us, and what the universe wants to bring through them, is the next frontier.

And why not? We've got this infinite beingness that's encapsulated in a human body, and the natural world has its own superpowers. One is not

Part Three

more important than the other. Activating all our senses and abilities to connect with all of the other life force energies that we share this planet with is something we're still figuring out. Yet, as we learn to live with the wisdom of our ancestors in the context of advances we've made in our current times, something profound is happening with our human evolution. Because we are wired to receive intuitive messages and have a connection with the natural world, our individual capacities are expanding. We're moving away from this notion of needing to have a guru or expert telling us what to do.

As with any relationship, there are things we can do to deepen our connection with the natural world. Implementing the following practical aspects of showing your support for nature will serve to support and nurture this profound interrelationship.

CHECK YOUR VIBE

The more we raise our vibration, the easier it is to connect to our natural state. Think of an old-fashioned radio where you turn the knob to tune into a particular station. You can tell when you're getting closer but there is still static. When you finally land on the correct station, it comes through loud and clear.

That's why the first foundational piece in connecting with nature is to observe your overall energetic vibration. Where are you vibrating? What are you putting in, on, and around you? Is the television blaring doom-and-gloom news in the background right now or is a lovely piano sonata on your music app? Reflect on that for a moment—does it feel like high or low energy?

Do a simple audit of your thoughts. Where are they vibrating? Are they in an emotion of love or fear? If you're thinking something more than three times or speaking it out loud, pay attention because a vibrational thread is going through these thoughts and words.

Now look around your home environment. Are you using synthetic products full of chemicals on your body and in your house? Do you smell the rain outside your window or the artificial scent of wall plug-ins? Diffusing essential oils that were responsibly cultivated is a good way to raise your vibration because you're infusing plant essences into your living space. The idea is to reduce the toxic load on your energy field because everything is energy.

Our bodies are amazing conduits to receive messages from nature. As with any conduit, you want to make sure you have a pure, clear channel. What we put into our bodies is so vitally important because it can affect our ability to receive messages from the natural world. Therefore, it's important to consider how you are refueling your physical body. The cleaner you eat, the clearer your intuitive channel will be. Eliminate pesticides, herbicides, preservatives, artificial sweeteners, food dyes, fluoride, and other chemically derived processes as much as possible. Choosing organic is beneficial for your body as well as the planet. Personally, when I'm deeply listening and tuning in, I adopt more of a plant based, raw food diet of high-vibrational foods.

Increasing your personal vibration starts with adopting an attitude of gratitude. Being reverent and thankful for the good things in life and the abundances that we do have, even if things are not perfect or where we want them to be, will allow for even more abundance to show up. This applies to our interactions with nature as well. Whenever I'm working with a tree, plant, stone, or other element in the natural world, I always begin the interaction with a prayer of gratitude. I thank that flower, lake, or landscape for playing with me and giving me essential things for my survival, like oxygen. I express appreciation for its beauty and intelligence, just as I would a human being.

Gratitude is the easiest way into working energetically with the trees, plants, rocks, and landscapes because it takes away any kind of agenda, allowing interactions to just flow. So, even before you leave the house to go out in nature, check your vibe by doing these things to create the highest frequency in preparation for it.

ASK PERMISSION

As you begin to deepen your relationship with nature, it's important to ask permission to collaborate with whatever sentient being you want to work with. Remember my shopping mall analogy? Well, you wouldn't just walk up to a stranger and start talking to them without first saying, "Excuse me, may I ask you a question?" Being in a reciprocal relationship with nature simply begins with asking the tree, plant, or stone, *Can I work with you? Do you wish to work with me?* Trust that you will intuitively see, hear, or feel the answer.

In our excitement to connect with nature, we sometimes forget our manners. When I first started tuning into nature early on and somewhat unconsciously collected stones, twigs, flowers, and other plants, it dawned on me that I never asked a single one of those beings if they wanted to be moved from their native places or if they were willing to come home with me. Now, I always ask before picking a flower or putting a rock in my pocket.

Does that rock want to leave its home and the ecosystem it is accustomed to? How do we know what the answer is? Since the natural realm doesn't talk to us in the way that we communicate with other humans, we need to shift our awareness and perceptions to receive the messages being sent to us. You connect with the other being by dropping into your heart space. You use your breath, which is life force energy in the form of the element of air, in a slow, full, and complete rhythmic breath cycle, taking in the air through your nose for a count of four, holding it for a count of four, and then slowly and completely releasing it through your mouth for another count of four. You can even use sound with the release to help you move that energy that tends to get stuck in our bodies. Pause at the bottom of that exhale for a count of four and repeat the cycle for a total of four times. This intentional use of the life force energy through the breath activates heart coherence. Once this coherence is activated, it acts as a portal to the quantum field where we are connected to all things.

Through this act of dropping into the heart space, we connect with the aspect of nature in question and ask if we have permission or if this other being has any interest in working with us. If you feel lighter or drawn forward, this is a yes. If you feel heavier or repelled back in any way, this is a no. Depending on where you are in the process of your intuitive development, you may audibly hear an answer or see the word "yes" or the word "no" in your mind's eye. Or you may see the color green that indicates moving forward or the color red telling you to stop.

BRING AN OFFERING

In various earth-based traditions around the world, it is customary to make an offering to the natural world as a gesture of respect and gratitude for its wisdom. Sage, cedar, tobacco, and sweetgrass are commonly used herbs for this purpose. Make sure they have been sourced with integrity in a natural, organic, and sustainable manner. If these plants are not available, birdseed can be substituted.

Once you have gathered your offering, take a pinch of the herb or seed and hold it to your heart. With an intentional prayer, infuse the offering with gratitude for the cycle of life and your interconnectedness. If you have no physical offering, simply say a prayer or heart-based intention. This practice brings you into your heart space and honors the importance of the sacred relationship between humans and Mother Nature.

CONSIDER NATURE'S POINT OF VIEW

Remember that every element of nature is in process with their own lives as well. Part of coming into greater coherence with whole life consciousness is realizing that it's not about humans being at the top and everything else below. Instead, we're in this synergistic, holistic circle of life together. We are not less or more than a plant, rock, lake, or field.

Now, we pick up a seashell or rock, taking it out of its ecology without a second thought. But when we know better, we do better, and that's the whole point. When we bring consciousness to what we're doing, we approach nature in a different way. I think of tree trimming as being like a haircut; it doesn't hurt physically. When we have to trim a tree or take down a diseased tree, we can talk to the tree involved and the surrounding trees and tell them, *This is what's going on, this is what's going to happen, this is what you're going to hear, this is what you're going to experience,* so they know. I think twice about picking a flower or moving a stone from its habitat. I don't need to own that rose or crystal. I can enjoy it in a different way.

LISTEN ATTENTIVELY

The more we think about the natural world from a different point of view, the more it will begin to direct you. The next step is listening deeply, attentively, and waiting patiently to observe what comes through.

I spent two years under the tutelage of some trees. I'm normally an avid reader, especially on the topics of science and spirituality. I was told very specifically from the trees, *No more reading on anything about trees for a while.* So, I started listening to trees. Each day, they imparted some information, giving me some exercises and things to contemplate. They told me where to hold my classes and what information to share. At the end of the two-year period, I had these different bits and pieces. And when I compared it to what science and the arborists were writing about trees, I found it was the same thing.

To begin listening, release any expectations with a big exhale so you can receive whatever wants to come through. Do you see an image in your head that's most likely coming from this tree? Are you feeling a sensation? Is there a knowingness that drops in? Are you hearing something, whether you can translate it or not?

Listening to nature is very much like mediumship. When someone has a natural predisposition of hearing those souls who are no longer embodied in the physical, it's like they're a little light attracting those souls. Certain souls go to that light because they know, *You can hear me, you can see me.* With nature spirits, it's the same thing. They know you've got that open heart.

You can also think of connecting to the trees, stones, and plants as similar to traveling to another country and experiencing different cultures. After a while, you get comfortable there and begin understanding the language and nuances of that part of the world.

When near a group of stones or a tree or you're sitting on the bank of a river or looking at a mountain, drop into a heart space and engage life force energy through the breath. Take long, slow, rhythmic breaths. It moves us out of the head space of strategizing and trying to figure everything out and activates heart coherence. This allows us to enter the quantum field full of possibilities.

If you want to move to a new location or home, go talk to your trees. Ask them to connect you to the trees on your new property, the new place where you're going to continue your journey. I've done that multiple times

Part Three

and they've never steered me wrong. When I show up at the new property, I don't even notice the normal things that people do, I notice the tree. I say, "Oh my gosh, that's the tree they've been introducing me to." And soon, it's like having a friend helping me.

There's so much that the natural world can teach us when we take the time to listen. Following the simple steps that I've outlined here can help you expand your connection to the Divine through the natural realm in a profound way. When we remember and engage with earth energy, we are able to be in sacred alliance with life force energy as it expresses itself as the directions, the elements, the animals, the plants, and the minerals.

I invite you to invoke this alliance with the natural realm to amplify your manifestations and shapeshift the energy in your current circumstances, bringing you into a deep relationship with your Divine nature.

FINAL THOUGHTS AND BLESSINGS

*A*ncient indigenous cultures had specific medicine men and women—the seers, listeners, and dreamers—who traveled into the astral realm to receive higher wisdom and information for their tribes. Generations throughout time have been inspired and nurtured by these wisdom traditions, and now we're starting to open this knowledge to us all.

We're at a crucial tipping point in our development on the planet where we sincerely need a critical mass to be listening deeply to nature's wisdom. We require seers within our own families and communities, while embracing the truth that we are one global community, connected by the web of life. When we are in concert with the natural world, we can feel what resonates for us as our truth. Each of us is on a different path and opening more fully to our connection with nature is one of the many, multi-layered aspects of us moving forward in a new and more empowered way for our species.

Reconnecting with the earth energies isn't only about our planetary journey; it's about our soul's journey. As evidenced by the population on our planet alone, we're now entering a time in which more and more souls are remembering that we are Spirit in human form. Many more of us are desiring into unity consciousness, not just with each other but with nature and Divine intelligence.

Now is indeed our time of remembrance, the era about which countless ancient teachings have spoken. The natural world has always been calling us from deep within to do this. Finally, we are prepared to listen with our whole being and recall our true nature.

It is my prayer and intention that the stories shared in this book bring about remembrance and shifts in perception that help empower you and your relationship with the natural world. Engage with the aspects of what resonates for you and get clear about what the natural world is showing you. The deeper our respect and relationship with the natural world, the deeper the revelations we receive from them. What's waiting to be revealed to you? Your purpose? Your passion? Inspiration for your creativity? Peace of mind? Healing for your body and mind? Inspired guidance for the next steps in your life? The possibilities are infinite.

Join me in shifting from doing things to nature to being in collaboration with the natural realm and discover the messages, magic, and healing that are waiting for you.

Come outside, *nature's waiting…*

APPENDIX

Building Your Personal Tree, Flower, and Rock Symbology Library

TREE SYMBOLISM

Below you will find the predominant energy present in some of my favorite trees.

ASPEN
Determination
Overcoming Fear and Doubts
Transformation

BEECH
Patience
Tolerance
Community
Knowledge of the Past

BIRCH
Adaptability
Healing and Cleansing
Pioneering and New Beginnings
Courage
Renewal
Vision Quests

CYPRESS
Understanding Sacrifice
Security

Appendix

ELM
Strength
Intuition
Stability

JUNIPER
Spirit Realms
Integrity
Healing

MAPLE
Balance
Promise
Practical Magic
Versatility

OAK
Courage
Power
Strength
Protection
Wisdom

PALM
Peace
Tranquility
Protection
Opportunity

PINE
Healing
Balancing Emotions
Eternal Life
Persistence
Adaptability

SEQUOIA
Ancient Wisdom
Attaining Full-Potential
Longevity

WILLOW
Magic
Learning from the Past
Inner Visions
Dreams
Emotional Balance

FLOWER SYMBOLISM

Here is the symbolism for some of the common flowers and a couple plants that I work with in my practice.

ALOE – Brings soothing and healing to irritations, physically and energetically
DAFFODIL – Assists with clarity of thought
DAISY – Invitation to connect to the elemental realm
DANDELION – Encourages you to find beauty where you haven't looked

FERN – Open your heart to connecting with the elemental realm, especially the faeries

GARDENIA – Brings emotional protection or healing

GLADIOLA – Encouragement to pursue higher aspirations

IRIS – Infusion of peace and harmony

JASMINE – Invites you to pay attention to your dreams

MUSHROOM – Go into the stillness, listen, and try a different approach

ORCHID – Balancing your energies

PEONY – Possibility for healing mind, body, and spirit, as well as creative expression

ROCK SYMBOLISM

Here you will find common stones in each of the three main rock types. Understanding basic rock classification helps us choose which stones may be the best collaborators for specific needs. You can use this as a quick reference guide for the stones presented.

IGNEOUS ROCKS: All rocks begin their journey as igneous rock. Igneous rocks, from the Latin word for fire, form when hot, molten rock crystallizes and solidifies. The melt originates deep within the Earth near active plate boundaries, or hot spots, then rises toward the surface. Igneous rocks are divided into two groups, intrusive (cooling underground) or extrusive (cooling above ground), depending upon where the molten rock solidifies.

Basalt
Comes from spewed lava rather than lava flows
Root Chakra
Physical and Mental Strength

Courage

Calms Emotions

Ignites Creativity

Dolerite

Also known as Diabase, Bluestone, or Sarsen

Root and Solar Plexus Chakra

Emotional and Spiritual Healing

Standing in Your Truth and Courage

Helpful with Past Life Regression

Granite

Root and Sacral Chakra

Protection and Strength

Relationship Balancing

Strengthens Hair, Muscles, and Bones

Note: Red Granite is high in quartz, silica, and iron, mirroring the human body's bones and blood. Used frequently in ancient sites, temples, and churches

Obsidian

Root and Solar Plexus Chakra

Volcanic Glass

Psychic Protection

Shields Negativity

Emotional Healing

Helps Break Negative Attachments

Appendix

METAMORPHIC: The mantra of this rock group is, "Transformation!" Metamorphic rocks are rocks that have changed form due to heat and pressure. Metamorphic comes from the Greek words *meta*, meaning "change" and *morph*, meaning "to change form." Metamorphic rocks were once sedimentary, igneous, or even other metamorphic rocks that have been changed by heat and pressure.

Gneiss
Pronounced "nice"
Feminine
Solar Plexus Chakra
Blocks Negative Energy
Self-Confidence
Vitalizes Energy

Marble
Comes from limestone
Crown Chakra
Potential and Vision
Meditation
Recall of Dreams

Schist
Formed when bedrock moves
Root and Heart Chakra
Strength of Will
Overcoming Challenges
Flexibility
Self-Confidence

Changes Stagnation

Overcoming Negativity

Soapstone
Crown, Heart, and Root Chakra
Soothing
Releases Old Habits and Patterns
Readiness for Change
Amplification

SEDIMENTARY: Sedimentary rocks are formed from pre-existing rocks or pieces of once-living organisms. They form from deposits that accumulate on the Earth's surface. Sedimentary rocks often have distinctive layering or bedding. Many of the picturesque views of the desert Southwest show mesas and arches made of layered sedimentary rock. Sedimentary rocks assist us in coping with change over time.

Limestone
Root Chakra
Purification
Encourages Healing
Positive Thinking
Grounding and Centering

River Rocks
Assorted types of rocks shaped by the constant flow of water
Sacral and Third Eye Chakra
Restores Flow
Grounding

Peace
Prosperity

Sandstone
Sacral Chakra
Creativity
Truth and Clarity
Ease with Change
Balance
Flow

Shale
Root Chakra
Calms Emotions, used as a Worry Stone
Productivity
Perseverance

MEET OUR SACRED STORYTELLERS

JACK ALLIS is an author and spiritual teacher whose books and DVDs discuss how to create the new world, in these times of a paradigm shift, in accordance with the model of the world's indigenous people.

CHRIS BACHMANN is a Swiss-born world traveler, host of international extreme sport events, translator for indigenous tribes, and founder of the SuddenRush Guarana project. He lives within the Atlantic Rainforest in Bahia, Brazil.

A.K. BAKER is an avid outdoorsperson who gains immense enjoyment from connecting to nature.

REV. KIMBERLY BRAUN is a minister, spiritual teacher, and lifelong adventurer in the world of self-realization. She has been a Carmelite nun for 11 years and has traveled the world inspiring others. kimberlybraun.com.

FLORENTINE BISSCHOPS, L.L.M., is a licensed spiritual-intuitive elder and healer, animal communicator, and shamanic practitioner based in the Netherlands. She assists her international clients (animals and humans alike) in shifting and healing their emotional wounds. bubblesforyoursoul.com.

DAN CAVANAUGH has a passion for spending time in nature and photographing unique tree spirits. His mission is to share his renewed sense of wonder and joy with the world, one tree spirit at a time. He resides in Pittsburgh, Pennsylvania with his wife, Donna, and their son, Joey. treespiritsamongus.com.

ANNE CEDERBERG is a professional naturalist, artist, and writer. Her mission is to help others see the God in nature. She lives in Florida.

LYNNE D. CHOWN is a multifaceted explorer of conscious creation, subtle energy fields, ageless wisdom, and how matter becomes animated. This search has taken her on many wonderful adventures.

BYRON EDGINGTON is a retired commercial pilot and an award-winning author of five books, including *Journey Well: You Are More Than Enough*. He lives and writes in Iowa City, Iowa.

CHERI EVJEN concluded a corporate career and began her second act as a certified spiritual life coach, author, certified grief recovery specialist, and an ordained minister who helps fellow grandparents of child loss. She is enjoying her newfound love of drumming.

DAVE EYERMAN is a shamanic practitioner, licensed acupuncturist, and life coach. He helps people reconnect with their most authentic, natural, and spiritual self. daveeyerman.com.

JOHN PAUL (EAGLE HEART) FISCHBACH is a theatre and film director, initiated shaman, sacred pipe carrier, and site whisperer. His documentary series, *The Shaman and the Stones,* is currently in production.

VICTORIA ANN GLOD had a powerful incident with a dying animal that catapulted her into animal communication. She does Spiritual Response Therapy, a soul clearing that removes discordant energies and programs that keep us stuck in old patterns.

YSETTE ROCES GUEVARA, PH.D. gardens in co-creative partnership with Nature in New York's Hudson Valley. She works with humans who wish to know the Self, rejoin the web of life, and take their place at the table of creation. Find your center. Surrender to mystery. Step into mastery. mindsonfire.org.

ANN MARIE HOLMES is an author, environmental intuitive, and former member of the Findhorn Community in northern Scotland. She has worked as a consultant and teacher for more than 30 years. earthspiritspaces.com

TAMARA KNOX, M.MSC, PH.D., PSYTHD. is a bestselling author and enthusiast of theocentric psychology. She uses breath, sound, movement, consciousness, and food energetics to explore metaphysical and multidimensional realms. shekhinahpath.com.

JILL LANDRY has always felt a special connection with animals and nature. With a love for both science and creative pursuits, she enjoys sharing with others through teaching and writing.

BROOKE MAROLDI is an award-winning filmmaker, storyteller, playwright, and actress. She is certified as an intuitive strategist through the Academy for the Soul. Her affinity for trees, rocks, and fairies began early in life. Brooke lives and works in Nashville, Tennessee.

PATRISHE MAXWELL is a writer, speaker, and spiritual coach based in Canada. Her passion is helping others find their way back to their true selves so they can live abundant lives in harmony with nature.

MARY E. MCNERNEY is a corporate lawyer and author of the bestselling book *Earth Speaks Up*, which provides dynamic new perspectives on Earth and humanity's role here. Mary now speaks and teaches about communicating with Earth, the angelic realm, horses, and all of nature. marymcnerney.com.

KATE NELIGAN is a bestselling author, TEDx speaker, animal communicator/healer, creator of Awakening With Equines training/certification, and an equine-partnered life/business coach who pairs spiritual psychology tools with the intuitive healing power of horses. kateneligan.com.

JYOTI NOEL is an artist, weaver, teacher of children's reiki and animal reiki, children's storyteller, Waldorf School handwork teacher, and a grandmother.

REV. ARIEL PATRICIA is founder and CEO of Sacred Stories Publishing and Media, an ordained interfaith minister, and a leader in the fields of publishing, broadcasting, online learning, and conscious business. She is the author of five books and a sought-after speaker across multiple media platforms. Ariel served as a sergeant in the U.S. Marine Corps.

KAREN B. SHEA is an author, photographer, and nature lover. Her desire to teach children about the natural world led to publishing her book, *Clark the Mountain Beaver and His Big Adventure!* She is a passionate advocate for the environment and continues to use her skills to inspire others about this amazing world. clarkthemountainbeaver.com.

TRACY SHEPPARD, M.A. is a highly sensitive empath, healer, teacher, and author of the eBook *Free Yourself from Fear: The Fear Rocks and How They Help.* tracysheppard.com.

SHARON M. SIRKIS, B.S.N., is an accredited T'ai Chi Chih teacher, certified chakra energy healer, black belt, and a firekeeper and singer for Sundance and Native American sweat lodge ceremonies.

MARIAN S. TAYLOR, ED.D. began her career as an elementary teacher and retired as a university professor. She developed reading specialists, directed the university laboratory school, and served as chairperson of a university department. marianstaylor.com.

LINDA VAROS is a lifelong spiritual and natural world mystic, clairvoyant-medium guide, artist, author, Ecology Art Therapy instructor, and LMT and energy medicine master teacher.

MEET OUR FEATURED AUTHOR

ANA MARIA VASQUEZ is a multi-sensory animal and nature intuitive, and a shamanic practitioner. As a natural energy reader, she lifts the veil between what's occurring in the physical world and the energetic patterns behind it.

Through teaching, speaking, and remote sessions, Ana Maria's profound connection with the natural world sources her in helping others understand the spiritual messages coming from the animals and nature. She guides others in unpacking their intuitive skills so that nature can speak more clearly through them. Ana Maria is also a certified intuitive strategist and a Sacred Stories Luminary. She serves on the faculty of Academy for the Soul.

Learn more at intentiontraining.com